GOD-GOVERNED LIFE

GOD-GOVERNED LIFE
IN THE PSALMS

Dennis Gillett

THE CHRISTADELPHIAN
404 Shaftmoor Lane
Hall Green
Birmingham B28 8SZ

2010

First published 2010

ISBN 978-0-85189-191-0

Cover artwork:
Jamin Lean

Printed and bound in Malta by:
Gutenberg Press Limited

CONTENTS

FOREWORD

"O how love I thy law! it is my meditation all the day." (Psalm 119:97)

THE Psalmist meditated constantly on God's law, and therefore much benefit can be gained from carefully considering his conclusions. Many of the psalms reveal the struggles of godly individuals as they tried to uphold divine principles in a sinful world. Some were able to look back and see how their lives had been in God's hand at all times. Others remembered the times they had acted as if He were not there.

The Psalmist drew great encouragement from these experiences. He saw the wonder of God's purpose, and how individual believers can become associated with it. He saw the frailty of human nature, and God's compassion towards our weaknesses. He saw the power of sin, and rejoiced in the divine answer that makes sin powerless.

To live away from God leads only to death. To live in the knowledge of His purpose requires that men and women place their lives in His hands, acknowledging that He will direct their paths. When the things of God rule in the human heart, life becomes governed by God.

Such thoughts, drawn from various psalms, formed the basis of a series of addresses that were prepared twenty-five years ago as Bible School talks by Brother Dennis Gillett. They were meditations on the power of God as it can apply to the lives of individual believers.

Recordings of the series have been available for many years, but the material is produced now in printed form for a wider audience. The careful analysis of God's word contained here will help all who love God's law, and reveal the benefits to be gained from meditating constantly upon it.

MICHAEL ASHTON
Birmingham
November 2010

1

THE SECRET THINGS REVEALED
PSALM 25

THIS work is concerned with one predominant idea: the working of God's influence in the lives of His people; the way in which He, willing and doing of His good pleasure, has drawn close to them in the everyday experience of their living. Mysteriously, imperceptibly, incisively, He has drawn close. He has checked, He has guided, He has led, He has drawn, He has covered, He has protected, chastened, for love's sake. In short, He has moved in their experience in such a way that by their response to Him they have become God-governed. That is to say, they have become true Israelites.

God-governed

Now you may be thinking to yourself, quietly, that's a strange way to describe people – God-governed – a strange way of describing the experiences of discipleship. But it has a very special purpose, because the meaning of the word, Israel, is 'God-governed'. Notwithstanding what you may have heard to the contrary, that is its meaning: *El*, the word for God, and *Yisra*, governed, mastered. It is not a case of mastering God – no man masters God. The right experience is to be mastered *by* God, to be governed by Him. Hence this was the experience of Jacob at Peniel, to justify the change of his name from Jacob, heel-catcher, to Israel, God-governed. He was broken so that he could be healed, he was beaten so that he could triumph, he was mastered so that he could exult and be made a prince with God. In the day that a man submits to God, that is the day of his power with God.

This became the experience of Jacob, and it became the experience of Jacob's descendants. Their lives in some sense became God-governed, and this study is concerned to observe their experiences, in particular in the experience of the Psalmists. That is, to look at certain psalms where the idea of being God-governed predominates, to understand the original meaning of the psalm as far as we can, and then to make some application of it to our own experience and discipleship. It is not a complete study of each psalm; not a verse-by-verse exposition, but an attempt to fix on the predominant idea in the psalm, try to expose it and then try to apply it.

Psalm 25

One of the outstanding things about this psalm is how sad a song it is. Some of the words almost seem to be sobbed out: desolation, affliction, distress, travail, shame and pain. The circumstances in which it was written are evidently most sad and most sorrowful. The writer seems to be beset on every side with difficulty and distress. He is crushed by temptation, he is beset by sin, in danger from enemies, enduring pain and affliction. It is a very sad song, and yet here is a strange thing: although it is a sad song, it is not a song of despair. You will notice the singer rises above the frailties of the situation, and gives us a song of confidence and hope.

Notice that the first seven verses and the last seven verses seem to be in the form of a prayer; the centre portion is a kind of statement of faith in the goodness and power of God:

> "Good and upright is the LORD: therefore will he teach sinners in the way. The meek will he guide in judgment: and the meek will he teach his way. All the paths of the LORD are mercy and truth unto such as keep his covenant and his testimonies. For thy name's sake, O LORD, pardon mine iniquity; for it is great. What man is he that feareth the LORD? Him shall he teach in the way that he shall choose. His soul shall dwell at ease; and his seed shall inherit the earth. The secret of the LORD is with them that fear

> him; and he will shew them his covenant. Mine eyes are ever toward the LORD; for he shall pluck my feet out of the net." (Psalm 25:8-15)

This man, in spite of his pain and his difficulty, has been able to triumph over all these forces; his psalm of sorrow is turned into a song of confidence and victory. In the darkness of his life, he has been able to lift his face to the light. And if I am not mistaken, his face is radiant with hope and triumph. That is the spirit of the psalm we shall consider.

The secret of the Lord

This is just what we want to discover: what was it that enabled this man to be as he is revealed in the psalm? How did he come to this condition that he was able to triumph over all his difficulties and sorrows? There is a message here for all who are sorrowful, all who are sad, all who need comfort; for those who need encouragement. The answer – possibly – is somewhere in Psalm 25 if we are able to discover it. After pondering the psalm a great deal, I have reached the conclusion that the secret, the answer, might be in that central portion, and in the statement of faith in verse 14. In that verse perhaps is the clue:

> "The secret of the LORD is with them that fear him; and he will shew them his covenant."

If we can discover what this means, we might have the reason for this man's triumph, and the message for ourselves of comfort and encouragement. Dwell first on the word "secret". We read in scripture that "the secret things belong unto the LORD" (Deuteronomy 29:29), meaning literally 'the hidden things' – things known to God, but which cannot be made known to man at this stage. God knows they might be known to men one day, but not now, for they are veiled things that have not yet been revealed. There are such things, for Moses tells us so, and adds by contrast that, "those things which are revealed belong unto us and to our children for ever, that we may do all the words of this law."

Those secret things that belong to the Lord could not be known then by the people of Israel, but one day perhaps they will. The word used in Psalm 25 for "secret" is not one that describes the idea of Deuteronomy 29:29. We must therefore look at other places where it is used, to come to the fulness of its meaning, unveiling its significances and its underlying feelings:

> "Praise ye the LORD. I will give thanks unto the LORD with my whole heart, in the council (assembly, KJV) of the upright, and in the congregation."
> (Psalm 111:1, RV)

> "We took sweet counsel together, and walked unto the house of God in company." (Psalm 55:14)

> "For the perverse is an abomination to the LORD; but his secret (margin, or counsel; or friendship) is with the upright." (Proverbs 3:32, RV)

> "He that goeth about as a talebearer revealeth secrets: but he that is of a faithful spirit concealeth the matter." (Proverbs 11:13, RV)

Bringing together these different meanings and underlying flavours we shall discover the richness of the word used in Psalm 25: "council", "counsel", "friendship", "secrets".

Perfect harmony

The idea in Psalm 111 is of a company of persons sitting together in complete unity, separated from strangers and influences which corrupt and disrupt, having one heart and one purpose: in absolute agreement with each other. As far as we know, only once in human history has there ever been such a gathering. It was on the Day of Pentecost, when the disciples were all together, with one mind and one accord, with one heart and one spirit, under the control of the Lord himself, and having a passion to obey him (Acts 2:1). The absolute purity of the infant church, sad to say, was soon lost and never regained.

But if we put that meaning back into Psalm 25, we learn that God sits in council, that is, in perfect union and complete harmony with them that fear Him. There are no arguments, no controversies. In looking carefully into this particular word, it is evident from what is revealed in the lexicons that "council" is the nearest to its original meaning. Perfect union because there is no discord, perfect harmony because there is no disagreement: a condition between God and those who sit with Him. It carries the meaning of restfulness. There is nothing to create disturbance, but instead there is a condition of perfect peace.

We can thus read Psalm 25:14 as, 'the council of the LORD is with them that fear Him'. This is highly suggestive of silent, mutual understanding. I heard a man say once that there is a friendship so close and so intimate that friends can sit together without the need to say anything: not a friendship that must be silent, but a friendship that can be silent, if it likes. You may have many acquaintances, but not very many close friends: just a few, perhaps, with whom you are perfectly safe in being silent. It could well be that in the spectrum of human relationships the last and the final sign of true friendship is this ability to be quiet together. You are compelled to entertain an acquaintance, you are obliged to talk, sometimes almost to the point of weariness. But friends will sit quietly, knowing there is no obligation, there is no controversy, no conflict, therefore nothing needs to be hidden or explained away. Sometimes the spirit is discerned in the serenity and calmness of their way of living. Something like this is discovered and submerged in this word "council": "The council of the upright, and in the congregation" – the assembly, the sitting together in harmony; a sitting together in silent mutual understanding.

In Psalm 55, the word was translated as "counsel", and introduces a slightly different thought. The silence spoken of in Psalm 111 is broken here. "Counsel" implies conversation – familiar conversation: a freedom of speech between friends who know and understand one another well enough to be silent if they wish, but well enough to converse openly and frankly if they need to. And they do it without fear or apprehension.

When friendship speaks that is able to be silent, it is likely to be very valuable, not producing rubbish or careless talk. It will be worthwhile and open. A fine definition of friendship was coined by Mrs Dinah Craik, a Victorian authoress:

> "Oh, the comfort — the inexpressible comfort of feeling safe with a person — having neither to weigh thoughts nor measure words, but pouring them all right out, just as they are, chaff and grain together; certain that a faithful hand will take and sift them, keep what is worth keeping, and then with the breath of kindness blow the rest away."
>
> (*A Life for a Life*, chapter 16; 1859)

That is the kind of speaking that arises out of a capacity to keep silence when it is right to keep silent, and to speak when it is right to speak. If you were to sit down today to make a list of people with whom you have that relationship, it is unlikely you would get writer's cramp! To be able to say what is in your heart fearlessly, and to know that your friend will blow away the chaff and keep only the grain – the blessed possibility of frankness without fear – that is what is bound up in this word "counsel".

The Psalmist calls it "sweet counsel", qualifying the thought. We talked and we spoke to each other, we spoke our minds to each other, saying what was in our hearts, and there was a freedom arising out of a perfect mutual understanding. The secret of the Lord is with the man who has no secret to hide and is not ashamed to tell all his trouble and all his failure, knowing that with the breath of kindness, the grain will be retained and the chaff will be blown away. That is "counsel".

Receiving advice and guidance

In Proverbs 3:32 the word has another meaning. This is not the silence of mutual understanding, or the freedom of speech and openness of conversation which comes from friendship realised at the very highest level. In Proverbs 3 the idea is of receiving advice and guidance:

> "The froward is abomination to the LORD: but his secret (i.e., his wisdom and his advice) is with the righteous." (verse 32)

People who are wise with God's wisdom are not likely to be froward. Because they fear with a reverential fear the One who has made them wise, they are likely to be changed by that experience:

> "He that goeth about as a talebearer revealeth secrets; but he that is of a faithful spirit concealeth the matter." (Proverbs 11:13, RV)

We are compelled to ask, What are secrets? Your minds may go back in a flash to your childhood, for secrets are things that often play a large part in childhood friendships. It used to be a demonstration of friendship when we were very young, that two friends in innocent childhood would seal their friendship with one telling the other a secret. And the shared secret was a bond between them of their friendship. Of course, it makes us smile now, for it seems so foolish. Perhaps, instead of smiling, the memory of it ought to make us weep, for when we grew up we forgot telling secrets because we thought no one could be trusted with them. We became close, confined, and introspective.

The secret of the Lord known and experienced

Would to God we could trust people now as we trusted them when we were children. The scripture says that God can tell His secret things to some people:

> "Shall I hide from Abraham that thing which I do? ... For I know him (implying that He could trust him) ..." (Genesis 18:17-19)

Abraham, the old-fashioned man of faith, knew something about God that Lot, the progressive, successful businessman was never able to discover. It was a secret that was not given to men to utter, and that secret became the force which changed him and drove him and glorified his life.

Now perhaps something like this happened to the man in Psalm 25. There is that kind of friendship where the closest confidences can be discovered and enjoyed.

Let us bring together the meanings attributed to this word “secret”: unity without any disagreement or controversy or argument; mutual conversation, hearing and answering, counsel, advice, guidance, loving instruction; a special insight into intimate things, special confidences poured out, secret things of the Lord. It means having somewhere to go in absolute confidence in times of sorrow and desolation and travail. It means being able to speak honestly and frankly. Sometimes when we speak to God, it may be as if we have our fingers crossed to some extent, our tongue in our cheek. Some men feign resignation towards God, when really in their hearts they are still rebellious. The man who knows the secret of the Lord will be able to pour out his rebellion into the listening ear of heaven, and the Lord of the universe will listen and will not be angry. That’s the teaching of this psalm.

He will not be angry – such is the quality of the friendship. The chaff will be blown away, and the grain will be retained. Is this not the teaching of Romans 8? We are revealed there as not being able to speak as we ought to speak, “but the Spirit itself maketh intercession for us with groanings which cannot be uttered” (Romans 8:26): in the silent meditation of His purpose, in the active word of prayer, in the counsel and guide of His precepts, in the circumstances of the way He has chosen, in the deep revelation of what He is like – such as came to Job, for example, in his experiences. The secret of the Lord was known: “I have heard of thee by the hearing of the ear: but now mine eye seeth thee” (Job 42:5). The secret of the Lord is known and is experienced.

Is there a disciple who in his deepest heart does not long for and seek and desire this experience? This is what the Psalmist had in mind, the blessing of which he spoke. To put it into the words of the New Testament, to "be able to comprehend with all saints what is the breadth, and length, and depth, and height; and to know the love of Christ, which passeth knowledge, that ye might be filled with all the fulness of God" (Ephesians 3:18,19). That is the New Testament counterpart of, "the secret of the LORD is with them that fear him; and he will shew them his covenant".

In order not to give a wrong impression, let nobody think this is written because the writer has experienced it. That is not the basis of this exposition. Rather it is an attempt to discover the experiences of the man in this psalm, and to understand why he triumphed over his sorrows. That is the blessing that he spoke of. Let us notice the condition that he prescribed for obtaining it: "The secret of the LORD is with them that *fear* him." What then is "fear" in this context?

There are two kinds of fear. There is what may be described as servile fear: a cringing fear, a terror of God, which often issues at last in deceit, in hatred and in ruin – a dread which has awful consequences. The man who has that kind of fear will never know the secret of the Lord, because that kind of fear is the very antithesis of the condition and the blessing that is here described. It is a contradiction of all that the blessing means as it is described in this psalm.

There is another kind of fear – not servile fear but filial fear. It is not so much a fear of what God may do to a son by way of punishment, but what the son may do to his father by way of grief: a fear of grieving the father. Two verses from Proverbs express this idea: "The fear of the LORD is to hate evil" (Proverbs 8:13); and "by the fear of the LORD men depart from evil" (16:6). Think back to Psalm 25 with that principle in mind: "The secret of the LORD is with them that fear him", that is, those that hate evil and those that depart from evil. For those there is the secret of the Lord. It is telling us that God's secret can never be discovered by the man who loves sin. No one reading these words will admit to loving sin. Yet men and women, even those who hate sin, can never altogether abandon it. A man can in many ways be utterly faithful, yet have a persistence in some doubtful thing which he will not give up: some secret passion which he knows to be doubtful but which is known to him alone, for which, and from which he will not depart; some crookedness, some moral dishonesty, some indulgence which he knows he ought to leave but he does not; some secret failure which he knows he ought to master, and which might master him. What about that?

If you are thinking, "this author seems to know this very well", you are right. He once gave an address on "The Deceitfulness of Sin". Afterwards a member of the audience said, "You gave us a good address on sin: you must have had a lot of experience of it". Sadly, what she said was true. Sin stands in the way of us knowing the secret of the Lord as well as we could. It is an impediment to the path of unveiling. There is a sense in which it makes a man have eyes, yet he sees not; he has ears and he is deaf to the word of his Lord. The spiritual sensibility of the man is blunted. It's not bad, but it's blunted in some place because we know that we do something that must grieve God. And we do it notwithstanding. Consequently, we are not able to discover the secret things as well as we could.

Let us return to the psalm with what we have discovered, and look at the words of that man again: "The secret of the LORD (that is, the real living, personal, positive friendship of God; the consciousness of the daily care of God and His guidance – that inestimable blessing) is with them that fear him." That is to say, it is with those who hate evil and depart from evil, and seek to be done with every known experience of it – that's the master condition – with those who love obedience and try to do it, come what may.

Now, this will be no revelation; it will not surprise us. Indeed, it is common amongst people who know the

Bible well. The Bible is always telling us that the secret of real spiritual knowledge is obedience. We may have learning and understanding, but the real secret of spiritual knowledge is obedience. It is seeking to know in order to obey. "To this man will I look, even to him that is poor and of a contrite spirit, and trembleth at my word" (Isaiah 66:2). God looks at such a man more intently than any other. Jesus said, "If any man will do his (God's) will, he shall know of the doctrine, whether it be of God, or whether I speak of myself" (John 7:17).

Light and darkness

Did you notice in the psalm that this man said, "the meek will he guide in judgment: and the meek will he teach his way" (Psalm 25:9). That is the secret: "The meek will he teach his way." "All the paths of the LORD are mercy and truth unto such as keep his covenant and his testimonies" (verse 10). It means that when we begin to uncross our fingers, scales will fall from our eyes. That is the condition of the promise. In New Testament words it is found from the pen of the Apostle John. He wrote of "walking in the light" (1 John 1:7). Have you considered this understanding of that sentence? We might say it means walking righteously, walking truly. And we would be right. But think of it like this: it means coming out into the light, and being recognised for what you are. If you are in the darkness you are hidden, and such things you have and do are hidden. Your character is hidden. But if you are walking in the light you are seen; you are known, you are keeping nothing secret. The purpose of light is to reveal: "Whatsoever doth make manifest is light" (Ephesians 5:13). The purpose of darkness is to conceal. John said, "If we walk in the light, as he is in the light, we have fellowship one with another" (1 John 1:7). If we are open with one another, and true with one another, the fellowship is real. But if we are in the dark and keeping things secret, and what others see of us isn't our real self but something manufactured, then the fellowship is, to say the best, paltry.

It means being real, walking in the light; it means not pretending any more. It means giving up window dressing; it means being honest with ourselves; it means putting things right which we know to be wrong; it means healing the breach with God's other children if we have any breaches, quarrels or wrong thoughts; it means risking our reputation for the sake of being free and true; it means letting Christ into the room marked 'Private'; it means letting him into that half-hour in the day when deep down we wish he wasn't there. For each one, it means some strangely different thing. It might mean changing the books on our bookshelf, giving up a friendship, putting away some cherished indulgence, ending some doubtful practice – perhaps some dishonesty. These are the things that halt us from knowing the secret things of the Lord. We live among these things day by day, and yet somehow never get to the secret of it. We see and see not, we hear and hear not.

"The secret of the LORD is with them that depart from evil": with them that stop grieving God. It is an unchangeable law, and perhaps the noblest declaration of it fell from the lips of the King himself when he said, "Blessed are the pure in heart: for they shall see God" (Matthew 5:8).

His covenant

We have thought of the condition, but finally we must think of the promise itself:

> "The secret of the LORD is with them that fear him; and he will shew them his covenant."

What is a covenant? A covenant is an engagement that is entered into. The covenant of God with His people is an engagement entered into with them, through Jesus Christ His Son. Jeremiah, the prophet of tears and lamentation, was the one who foresaw and described it in words that tell of the great and gracious covenant of God with His people:

> "This shall be the covenant that I will make with the house of Israel; After those days, saith the LORD, I will put my law in their inward parts, and write it in their hearts; and will be their God, and they shall be my people. And they shall teach no more every man his neighbour, and every man his brother, saying, Know the LORD: for they shall all know me, from the least of them unto the greatest of them, saith the LORD: for I will forgive their iniquity, and I will remember their sin no more."
>
> (Jeremiah 31:33,34)

God enters into this covenant with all that hate evil and want to depart from it with all their heart. They will find their way to Him and His promise through the one God has promised and appointed: the Anointed One, chosen to be Saviour and Judge; the Man of Nazareth, the Virgin-born.

The covenant promises pardon, peace and purity for all who fear with reverent fear the One who makes the promise – all the spiritual things which arise from a transformed mind and a regenerated spirit; the grace of God flowing out from His throne over all the life of men; the therapeutic forces of His government extending over the world that is war-weary, sin-laden, fear-filled, bringing to hearts that are broken and bereft the balm of God's infinite peace. All the things that enslave or hinder humanity are to be broken and ended. Men whose necks are bent to tyranny today will be men standing erect in the presence of the King; men who boasted of their freedom falsely, glad at last to be bondslaves of the king of kings. This is what the covenant means in its ultimate sense.

The realisation of this can nerve us in the day of battle. The hope of all these blessed things gives us hope in a hopeless world, encourages us in days that are dark and sad, gives us joy in our hearts when all around us is bitterness; it puts a spring in our step. The vision on the horizon is the source of our confidence. Thank God for the promise of His kingdom and of His government, and let us always cling to it with all our hearts and souls. But nevertheless and notwithstanding, let us at the same time look at it in a more present and personal way, because the realisation of the covenant is not wholly postponed until the age to come. The Psalmist says, "He will shew them his covenant". Do not mistake his words. The thought is not just that He will "shew them his covenant", making plain to them what the covenant is, or the meaning of its terms. It means much more. "He will shew them" means He will enable them to see the ratification of the covenant in their experience both now, and hereafter. I am careful to say "now". Because we are frail and fearful, because sometimes we have trembling hearts, because sometimes there are days when we wonder whether after all the covenant is sure and steadfast, because in the midst of our weakness sometimes our faith begins to falter, because sometimes we stumble on the pathway to life, because we say some days, 'Has God forgotten to be righteous?', or 'Will He show us any good?', then not long afterwards we are compelled in our shame to remember the words of Jacob: 'The God of the covenant has been with me all my days'.

From Marah to Elim

There will be readers of these words who once came to Marah and found there all its bitterness, thinking in their trouble they would never be the same again, but go softly all their days. Then they travelled on and at last they came to Elim, and they found rest. In their experience they came closer to the Lord their God. Perhaps those who have been in His fear the longest will know His secret the best. But like the Psalmist, the message of this study is that the sob of sorrow can become the song of salvation. This is an essential part of the God-governed life. "The secret of the LORD is with them that fear him, and he will shew them his covenant." May God grant that you will come to know more and more what that means in the oncoming days.

2

PARDON AND PEACE
PSALM 32

THERE are some things in Psalm 32 which, if they are looked at superficially, are difficult to understand. It's a psalm that needs to be read carefully several times in order to grasp the real significance of the teaching. When this is done, one of the first things that becomes evident is that this is not the attempt of a theologian to offer us a theory about sin and forgiveness. This man is not theorising, but is speaking out of the sorrow and joy of his own deep experiences. It's a song that sobs with sorrow and exalts with joy. Underlying the figures which the singer uses there are deep feelings of bitterness and disappointment; there are feelings of despair and loneliness. That is why its teaching is so valuable to us who perhaps want to share in that same common human experience. This man has passed through the valley, and through the great darkness, and at last he has come into the light. He stood in the presence of the great silence, and then at last came to hear the voice of assurance and of counsel. He has been overwhelmed with sorrow, but at last he has received wonderful succour.

A gasp of relief

This is no theory from a man who is writing a book; this is the timeless singing of a man who is familiar with the deepest things of sorrow and joy. To illustrate this, look carefully at the first verse:

> "Blessed *is he whose* transgression *is* forgiven, *whose* sin *is* covered." (Psalm 32:1)

Now that is the statement of a great truth, but rather prosaically spoken. It is not really what this Hebrew man said. Look at the verse again, missing out the words in italics which were added by the translators. When you do that there is no personal pronoun "he", and that is important. The singer is not speaking of "he" – some other man – he is not speaking of some composite man. What he really said was, "O, the blessedness of transgression forgiven and sin covered". It was the gasp of relief, not the declaration of a statement of faith; the lifting of a great burden. He was describing something God has done for him, when he was in the depth of despair, when he was in the midst of sorrow and silence. It's a doxology: a great expression of praise to God for deliverance which has come to this sorrowing man. Indeed, at the end of the psalm, you can notice the same note of praise:

> "Be glad in the LORD, and rejoice, ye righteous: and shout for joy, all ye that are upright in heart."
>
> (Psalm 32:11)

In between the opening praise and the closing praise, the Psalmist gives us reasons for praising altogether. He tells us of his feelings and his experiences. When there was no light upon the pathway, and when there was a great chillness in his soul – in those circumstances he was constrained to sing out, "O, the blessedness of transgression forgiven, and sin covered".

Aspects of failure

Notice in verses 1 and 2 that he speaks of "sin", of "transgression", and of "iniquity". Probably, these are all different aspects of his failure. Behind the word "transgression" is the idea of a conscious breaking of the law; a wilful going beyond the boundary; a trespass; a moving out beyond the law. On the other hand, underlying the word "sin" is the idea of missing the mark: of seeing the target, aiming at it, and missing it. When this word is used in non-Biblical literature of the time, the word used in this psalm and other places for "sin", it is used always to convey this idea – like a man who sits down to write a great epic poem, and when it is finished, he knows it is no epic. Or he has a great ideal and he seeks to live by it, but in his most honest moments he knows that he has fallen short of the ideal. In all those contexts, this is the word that is used: seeking to rise up to the standard, and to fail and fall short. It may be, of course, that your experience has never taken you into the realms of transgression. You may not know what transgression is: deliberately to break the boundary and flout the commandment. You may not have done that, but most will understand what is meant by "sin": to know the ideal, and to fall short of it.

The word "iniquity" as used in this psalm conveys the idea, not so much of the thing done, but the state of sinfulness which arises from the sin: a deterioration in character that issues from the disobedience. Iniquity is more of a condition than an act, but it arises from the act.

What this man tells us is that he knew the desolating power of all these aspects of failure. He knew that these are the things that harm and impoverish the soul of a man: the dark degenerating degradation that settles on a man's spirit when he is convicted of this kind of wickedness; the loneliness that hangs on his heart like an icicle, and makes him feel to be severed from all men, and from God as well.

The blessedness of divine judgement

So the Psalmist turns from his doxology to state the truth in relation to the individual soul: "Blessed is the man", he says, "unto whom the LORD imputeth not iniquity, and in whose spirit there is no guile". Ought we not to be thankful that he did not say, 'Blessed is the man to whom his neighbour imputeth not iniquity'. Your experience is likely to have taught you that it is a more blessed thing to be judged by God than to be judged by men; that it is easier sometimes to please God than it is to please men. The Psalmist had learned this: he discovered that God is more reasonable, more patient, and more just than men. He had learned that God's ways and works are always based on His absolute and perfect knowledge. One of the most wonderful things about the kingdom of God is going to be that the King shall not judge by the sight of his eyes or by the hearing of his ears; his judgements are to be utterly righteous. They will be based upon a perfect knowledge of all the underlying facts and forces, and all the invisible issues.

So it is with God and sin, and forgiveness. That's a comforting thought: a perfect knowledge of all the forces which are involved. It means that underneath the eyes of fire, there is the voice of love. The witness of prejudiced, faulty humanity is outlawed and excluded when a man stands in the presence of the great God of heaven to seek to be acquitted. The great difference between human judgement and divine judgement is that there is no need to fear that the judge is prejudiced. There is no need to be worried that the judge might be corrupted. And what will the judge do? The psalm tells us that He will acquit the guilty altogether; He will not impute any iniquity. The transgression, this man said, is forgiven; the sin is covered. But there is a condition. Far too often we hear people say that the forgiveness of God is unconditional. There is a condition, and it is something in the man: "Blessed is the man ... in whose spirit there is no guile" (Psalm 32:2). In other words, if guile is cast out by the man, God will cast out the sin. The vital question is, what really is guile?

"... in whose spirit there is no guile"

Guile means seeking to hide things, or to deceive. It means trying to cloak things over. On the face of it, it sounds ridiculous to suggest we can hide anything from God, deceive Him, or try to cloak things over in His presence. We are "naked and opened unto the eyes him with whom we have to do" (Hebrews 4:13). How foolish to try to hide anything from God; we cannot really deceive Him. No man in his right mind would try to practise guile in the presence of God. But we do! Some of the best men in the Bible tried it. David is an example: he practised guile with God. When he committed the sin with Bathsheba, he did his best to hide it, even to the extent of eliminating her husband.

How often then do we argue in our minds, and therefore in God's presence, that some evil thing is not really so very evil? How often do we seek to make plausible the wrong things in our lives, which we know we ought to shed but really we want to keep? How often do we seek, for reasons, or reasonable excuses, to justify our waywardness and our disloyalty? How often do we give high sounding names to doubtful things in order to make them more acceptable? Or how often do we just refuse to face the truth about ourselves? All these are guile or deceit: seeking to hide the true position.

The psalm tells us that where there is guile, God imputes iniquity. It is as though a man may sin, and in sinning he has fallen short of the mark, but the actual iniquity is imputed when that sinning man seeks to justify his failure by guile. The actual act is done, but in this final and awful sense the iniquity is marked on him, not at the moment he does the act but in his reaction afterwards, when he either resolves to repent at once, or to justify his action by some kind of guile. The man says, in that moment, when he insists on justifying his wrongdoing, the iniquity is marked. It is imputed when he justifies his failure by deceit.

By some plausible cloaking over, he seeks to make himself better than he is; he refuses to face the truth about it and at this point he is, as it were, found guilty by God. While he remains in that condition, the guilt is marked, and it cannot be moved. It is like in Macbeth: "Out, out, damned spot", and there is nothing to move it. The sin is sealed – by guile. Have you ever noticed the similarity between the words 'guile', and 'guilty'? Think about it.

On the other hand, if there be no cloaking over, if there be no hiding, no plausible arguing; if the man says, I will excuse the thing no longer, it's been hidden long enough, it never ought to have been hidden, it is wrong, I have sinned, God help me: then, in a moment, in the twinkling of an eye, swift as lightning is swift, like the first breaking of the sunlight, God pronounces on that man the verdict of the guiltless. This man affirms by the administration of the Holy Spirit that the man is acquitted; he is free, and in the freedom and relief which he discovers, he sings out, "O, the blessedness of transgression forgiven, and sin covered".

"Thy hand was heavy upon me"

What we should focus on now is a contrary experience, and the Psalmist dwells upon it: the experience of a man who knows he ought not to practise guile in the presence of the Lord, but nevertheless he does; who knows he ought to come out into the light, but instead he is hidden away, either for fear or for self-will. He is cloaking the evil, he is hiding the sin. This man who wrote the psalm had had the same experience, and he now tells us his feelings:

> "When I kept silence, my bones waxed old through my roaring all the day long. For day and night thy hand was heavy upon me: my moisture is turned into the drought of summer." (Psalm 32:3,4)

In effect he was saying, 'I put a bold face on it; in my bravado I tried to convince myself that God did not care, that He was invisible and indifferent. But there was no peace, and there was no life' – like Peter warming himself by the world's fire, but in his heart was a coldness which no fire lit by human hands would ever warm. Notice the figure which the Hebrew man uses: "my moisture was dried up, as in the drought of summer". Remember, he is describing his condition when he was practising guile, when he was trying to cloak the sin.

This is a picture of a tree, withering away because of dryness – dying for want of moisture. In Psalm 104:16 we read, "The trees of the LORD are full of sap". While that may be a very limited description of a tree, for it is full of much more than sap, it is full of beauty, colour and music. Lie under a great tree of a summer day; lie there quietly, and you will know that trees are more than full of sap. The word “sap” here covers a great deal. It means life, and beauty, and music, and fulfilment. It is like a man when he is right with God: life is full and free and wonderful. He is fulfilling his destiny, he is realising his manhood, he is what God intended him to be. When he is like this, he is like a tree full of sap.

But the man with sin hidden, the man with sin unconfessed, is like a tree dried up, half-dead, withered, without music – appearing respectable outside, but within soured, fevered, with no rest and no joy. This is the condition the Psalmist traces, and he traces it through the very activity of God: “Day and night thy hand was heavy upon me.” This sounds severe, but it is really the love of God in action. The man means that when he wanted to forget the reality of his sin, when he wanted to have it out of his mind and to be done with it, put it behind him and forget it; when he wanted to do that, then the Lord kept it alive in his consciousness and in his heart. The Lord didn’t allow him to get very far from the realisation of what he had done. He kept the consciousness of the iniquity before him. When we think the matter is best forgotten, and put behind us, this God of heaven sustains the controversy in our hearts, the sin, the habit, the enticement, which we know is wrong, but which we won’t confess. He lets it haunt us. God gives His children no rest in their waywardness, so that He can bring them out of their jeopardy into safety. He places obstacles in the path to halt their wilfulness. His “hand was heavy upon me”, says the Psalmist.

Two ways

He will not let us escape to destruction. It is the love of God that chastens us, as we know well. Whilst this thought is in mind, look at verses 8 and 9. There is a sudden change here, because by the strange and mysterious processes of inspiration, God has made the

Psalmist to speak the words of God Himself. These verses are God's words to him:

> "I will instruct thee and teach thee in the way which thou shalt go: I will guide thee with mine eye. Be ye not as the horse, or as the mule, which have no understanding: whose mouth must be held in with bit and bridle, lest they come near unto thee."
>
> (Psalm 32:8,9)

The closing words are confusing. You don't put bits and bridles on horses to prevent them coming near to you! They are used for the opposite purpose. The Revised Version translates the passage, "Be ye not as the horse, or as the mule, which have no understanding; whose trappings must be bit and bridle to hold them in, else they will not come near unto thee." This makes more sense.

Notice in the context of God's overriding care and guidance of His children, in this passage there are two ways a man may go. The first way is by understanding: "Be not as the horse, or as the mule, which have no understanding". God calls us to a condition of understanding, by an inward impelling motive which understands what the will of the Lord is, and finds delight in doing it. That is one way: an inward impelling motive of understanding. The other way, in verse 9, is by "bit and bridle": a compelling pressure from outside, from circumstances and incidents which curb and hurt and check and master, so that the powers of a man's life are realised at last, even through this chastening.

Jesus our Lord is the finest example of the first method, exemplified in one great sentence attributed to him: 'I delight to do thy will, O my God' (Psalm 40:8, Hebrews 10:7). Most others are examples of the other category.

Don't think, however, that the use of bit and bridle means the elimination of our will. Don't get it wrong. A mule, whose owner tries to control it by bit and bridle, still has a will of its own. But in the process of God's chastening, the effect of what He is doing changes our will gradually, bit by bit, step by step. The weaker will is mastered by the stronger will. Not that it is imposed so that we become automatons and puppets, but by the influences of the chastening, we begin to understand and move into the first category.

"I will confess ..."

Observe what the man tells us in verse 5 about the things which happened when he acknowledged his sin: "I said, I will confess my transgressions unto the LORD; and thou forgavest the iniquity of my sin." Doesn't it seem that the great God, according to this sentence didn't even wait for the actual confession to be made, but in the very moment the man resolved to confess, the Lord met him. "I said, I will confess ... and thou forgavest the iniquity of my sin". Now, this is how we ought to understand it, for it is in harmony with the New Testament. Think of the picture of the father in the parable of the Prodigal Son. Recall the story of the wandering boy who left home and came to deep degradation. When he came to himself, he resolved to return home and seek reinstatement as a servant in his father's house. The father was looking out every day into the distance with shaded eyes to see if the boy was coming home. Every day he was watching, hoping, anticipating that he might see the wandering figure of the child he had lost. Then it happened. One day, looking out again, he saw his son a great way off. The father didn't wait for him to come to the front door and plead for forgiveness. The lad was a great way off and the father ran, and fell on his neck and kissed him. That is utterly in harmony with Psalm 32: "I said, I will confess ... and thou forgavest the iniquity of my sin."

That's the true picture of God the Father. Any child of God out in the world, degraded by sin, burdened by transgression, cold with loneliness: if such a one at this very moment wherever they may be (God knows), will say 'I will confess my sin; I will arise and go to my father, and say "Father, I have sinned against heaven and before thee'" – the lesson of this psalm is that in that very moment, as the decision is made, God will grant pardon. God does not wait for the formalities to be fulfilled. He does not wait for the sabbath day, for the hour of bread breaking. He doesn't wait for the last hour of evening, but only for the moment when the heart casts aside the guile and turns to Him. When a man says, 'I will come to God as I really am; I will give up this business of hypocrisy, I will have no more of it' – at that moment the veil is broken down, and at that moment there is fellowship with God.

A hiding place in the midst of trouble

"Thou forgavest the iniquity of my sin." This explains the feelings which underlie the expressions of relief at the beginning of the Psalm: "O, the blessedness of transgression forgiven and sin covered." So when a man is guileless before God, he is delivered from sorrow. Notice verses 6 and 7:

> "Surely when the great waters overflow they shall not reach unto him. Thou art my hiding place; thou wilt preserve me from trouble; thou wilt compass me about with songs of deliverance." (RV)

This does not mean, and we should not understand it to mean, that there is a promise of freedom from sorrow or trouble always. It doesn't mean that the man of God thereafter will never be in difficulty, or (in a New Testament context) that the man of God will never be imprisoned. But it does mean that the sorrow will not master him; it means that the trouble will not overwhelm him. Though he is in prison he will be able to sing songs – not because the prison doesn't matter, but because he is a citizen of that city where there is no night. He can sing because he is pardoned and has peace.

The great waters have gone over them but they are not destroyed. In the midst of their troubles they found a hiding place, like the man said. They have been in the presence of great waters, but they weren't overwhelmed. They have been through troubles, but have found a place of refuge. Near to us in all the harm of circumstances is the love of God. That's what he is saying. We have listened to the whisper of His word, and we have taken courage. We have yielded to the constraint of His guidance and in that yielding we have been preserved. So, let us return to look at those two ways: the ideal, of inward compelling motive; and the other, the way of compelling pressure from outside. This is not say that the disciples of Christ are neatly packaged into one way or the other, for it isn't like that. Life is too complex for that. The truth surely is that most people are partly in one and partly in the other. Both ways in our lives are inextricably mixed up together; both having influences upon us. Today, perhaps, we are yielding freely, we are in the ideal way; then tomorrow we are under the constraint of bit and bridle.

The lesson to be learned is this: to the extent we refuse the first – to that extent we shall have to be under the influence of the second. If we will not have one, then God will seek to bring us to the other. This principle is revealed in the New Testament in 1 Corinthians 11, in the context of failure among the members of the Corinthian ecclesia:

> "For if we would judge ourselves, we should not be judged. But when we are judged, we are chastened of the Lord, that we should not be condemned with the world." (1 Corinthians 11:31,32)

There are the two conditions: "if we judge ourselves" is the ideal way; "but when we are judged, we are chastened" – that's the other way.

Think for a moment of the figure of the winepress. The purpose of the winepress is that, under the pressure applied, the inwardness of the grape will be revealed and the real purpose brought to completion. So it is in God's winepress. Under the pressure applied by Him, the inwardness of our life is brought out: we can be outwardly what we are inwardly, and step by step all His resources are realised and fulfilled eventually by this method. So by the conflicts and restraints of a God-governed life lived within the realm of Christ's commandments, a man or a woman may come at last, close to the ideal, by way of understanding. It may be through the other method, that is by way of chastening.

They are very often mixed up together. First of all it is daybreak, then it grows more and more unto the perfect day. So a man or woman gradually is ready to cancel the word 'duty' and find the word 'delight' in the doing of the Lord's will.

Falling short of the ideal

The confirmation of this interpretation is found expressly in two other Psalms, 39 and 40:

> "I said, I will take heed to my ways, that I sin not with my tongue: I will keep my mouth with a bridle, while the wicked is before me. I was dumb with silence, I held my peace, even from good; and my sorrow was stirred. My heart was hot within me, while I was musing the fire burned: then spake I with my tongue ... Deliver me from all my transgressions: make me not the reproach of the foolish ... Remove thy stroke away from me: I am consumed by the blow of thine hand." (Psalms 39:1-10)

This again is the picture of a man, called to the ideal, but failing or falling short of it; a man who has vowed a vow, but has not been able to keep his vow. He has been mastered by his own will, but even in that situation God is still with him; He has not forsaken him. Through the strange processes of chastening, God is seeking to recover this failing man. By a compelling pressure from outside, by the use of circumstances which check and hurt and curb, a man is mastered gradually and brought back to the path of rectitude, and the powers of his life are realised even through chastening and judgement:

> "Remove thy stroke away from me: I am consumed by the blow of thy hand. When thou with rebukes

dost correct man for iniquity, thou makest his beauty to consume away like a moth." (Psalms 39:10,11)

So God, appearing to be severe, is acting in love for the redemption of a failing man.

"Mine ear hast thou opened"

"I waited patiently for the LORD; and he inclined unto me, and heard my cry. He brought me up also out of an horrible pit, out of the miry clay, and set my feet upon a rock, and established my goings. And he hath put a new song in my mouth, even praise unto our God: many shall see it, and fear, and shall trust in the LORD. Blessed is that man that maketh the LORD his trust, and respecteth not the proud, nor such as turn aside to lies. Many, O LORD my God, are thy wonderful works which thou hast done, and thy thoughts which are to us-ward: they cannot be reckoned up in order unto thee: if I would declare and speak of them, they are more than can be numbered. Sacrifice and offering thou didst not desire; mine ears hast thou opened: burnt offering and sin offering hast thou not required. Then said I, Lo, I come: in the volume of the book it is written of me, I delight to do thy will, O my God: yea, thy law is within my heart. I have preached righteousness in the great congregation: lo, I have not refrained my lips, O LORD, thou knowest." (Psalm 40:1-9)

That is another picture of God's ways with sinners. Think again of the figure he uses of the ears open. Some people think it refers to the ancient Hebrew ceremony where the servant's ear is pierced by way of being affixed to the doorpost as a sign of his perpetual servitude to a master whom he loves. That may not be the meaning here, because of the way the psalm is quoted in Hebrews 10. The open ear in this case is an ear opened to be utterly attentive to God's will. When the ear was opened there came the declaration: "I delight to do thy will, O my God."

Furthermore, the idea of one ear being opened in the ancient ceremony of servitude is difficult when you notice the precise words here: "mine ears hast thou opened" (verse 6). The ears, both of them, were opened ready to obey. In fact, in Hebrews 10 the sentence is quoted differently. Instead of, "mine ears hast thou opened", the apostle writes, "a body hast thou prepared me" (Hebrews 10:5). It seems almost like a contradiction, but not really. The body prepared was a body with open ears. That was the preparation of the body: "mine ears hast thou opened"; a body that, despite all the forces that were besetting him enables him to say and mean: "I delight to do thy will, O my God". We therefore know that the delight was once perfectly revealed in this man of Nazareth. He was the inward impelling force: a condition where every act and every force is made captive to the purpose of God and the power of His word and His will. Along with the sweet constraint of love he was obedient unto death, yea the death of the cross. This was the God-governed life in all its perfection and all its fulness.

The atonement in daily life

Finally, there is one other aspect, for it is the continual argument of the New Testament writer, which we ought not to overlook. It is the pardon which comes to us through the love of God, in this way or that; the sacrifice of Christ which has been made for us for love's sake. This thing ought to have a practical effect upon our daily living. The atonement as presented to us in the New Testament is nearly always shown to have a practical effect upon our lives. Sometimes it is presented to us in theological terms, but mostly as something that will affect how we live. It ought to be doing something to us. In a way, the effect of the pardon we receive is manifested in how we behave, not only in some great momentous event in our lives, which occurs perhaps only once or twice. It is in the ordinary, commonplace things of the God-governed life that the effect of pardon is to be manifested.

Here are some examples:

"Husbands, love your wives, even as Christ also loved the church, and gave himself for it."
(Ephesians 5:25)

"Exhort servants to be obedient unto their own masters ... that they may adorn the doctrine of God our Saviour in all things." (Titus 2:9,10)

"For the grace of God that bringeth salvation hath appeared to all men, teaching us that, denying ungodliness and worldly lusts, we should live soberly, righteously, and godly, in this present world."
(verses 11,12)

The very best example is in 2 Corinthians 8. It's a chapter about money, and there are some who think that money is the very lowest form of service you can be engaged in, that money is pretty sordid. You may have heard the story of the ship that was in peril on the sea. It looked as if all would be lost, the sea was that rough. The captain was desperate and said to the first mate, 'We've done all we can from a seaman's point of view. It looks as though we shall be lost; we shall have to turn to God. Now I want you to go below and organise something religious'. So the first mate went below and took up a collection! We may think, what a foolish man to imagine that a collection was religious. But under certain circumstances a collection can be very religious indeed. It was in 2 Corinthians 8:

"Therefore, as ye abound in every thing, in faith, and utterance, and knowledge, and in all diligence, and in your love to us, see that ye abound in this grace also." (verse 7)

So the thing which some people think is pretty low and not to be mentioned, Paul calls a grace. And he equates it with knowledge and utterance and faith and diligence. He says, "see that ye abound in this grace also". The reason for drawing attention to this passage is the motivation. Why were they to abound in this grace, this commonplace thing of a collection for the saints? Why ought they to abound and be generous? Why? The reason is given in verse 9:

> "For ye know the grace of our Lord Jesus Christ, that, though he was rich, yet for your sakes he became poor, that ye through his poverty might be rich."

The everyday things of the God-governed life are set in relation to the noblest doctrines of our faith. The way we live in the daily round and the common task, is to be inspired by that life which was won out of death by the sacrifice of our redeemer. And the realisation of that and the pardon that comes from it is able to set us free and inspire us in the way that we live.

The principle is also to be seen in the first Corinthian letter, where again the apostle instructs them about money:

> "Now concerning the collection for the saints, as I have given order to the churches of Galatia, even so do ye." (1 Corinthians 16:1)

This comes immediately after the great fifteenth chapter, the wonderful discourse on resurrection: the chapter which focuses sharply on the final issues, which climbs to the very heights, which says that "Christ died for our sins according to the scriptures", and that if he never rose from the dead we are still in our sins, and of all men most pitiable. The chapter ends on the great doxology of joy and confidence:

> "O death, where is thy sting? O grave, where is thy victory? The sting of death is sin; and the strength of sin is the law. But thanks be to God, which giveth us the victory through our Lord Jesus Christ. Therefore, my beloved brethren, be ye stedfast, unmoveable, always abounding in the work of the Lord, forasmuch as ye know that your labour is not in vain in the Lord. Now concerning the collection for the saints ..."
> (1 Corinthians 15:55–16:1)

There it is, in the heart of one of the best and noblest declarations of our faith. So because of the atonement, and because of the pardon which comes from it, this ordinary thing is put into the full tide of your spiritual life. It is fixed in full relationship to the highest and the noblest doctrines of the faith; it is measured in the full light of the Lord's resurrection; it is motivated by that life which was won out of death, by the Son of God himself. Finally, think of the peace which comes through the pardon which is given to us, as David told us with a great sigh of relief: "O the blessedness of the man whose sin is covered". The reason he said it is something we know well in our deepest heart, that sin cuts a man off from God: it blinds his vision, it deadens his emotion, and it makes his will perverse; it fills his soul with guilt and mystery, it pollutes the very sources of life. It is like paralysis and powerlessness. A man wants not to sin, but somehow he does. In the words of Paul, "What I hate, that do I" (Romans 7:15). It is a confession of appalling weakness.

Now, the central mystery of the God-governed life is that in the midst of that perversion, and in the chaos of it there is pardon, and issuing from the pardon there is perfect peace – men finding God and finding themselves through this blood-shedding. I confess to you, I cannot fathom it. I have to tell you, I cannot measure it. I can only preach that through it there is peace. It defies analysis, it transcends explanation, but there are people who could tell you with shining faces that it is true. There is a quietness that comes into the God-governed life through the knowledge that God is peace. The blessedness of God comes upon those that are acquitted and their hearts are at rest; one small atom in this great universe, in harmony with God. Think of that.

No wonder then that David sang, "He that trusteth in the LORD, mercy shall compass him about" (Psalm 32:10).

3

REFUGE WITH THE GOD OF JACOB
PSALM 46

ONE of the outstanding features of these old Hebrew songwriters, underlying all their music, is the unalterable conviction that God is there, and will not be moved and that He is utterly dependable. Understanding all the reverses, the hardships, the perplexities, there is this unswerving and unabated confidence in God. Now this is the rock foundation on which they base their words, their music and their faith. And in Psalm 46, the expression of this confidence is most startling and most convicting.

Look again at the first three verses:

> "God is our refuge and strength, a very present help in trouble. Therefore will not we fear, though the earth be removed, and though the mountains be carried into the midst of the sea; though the waters thereof roar and be troubled, though the mountains shake with the swelling thereof." (Psalms 46:1-3)

It matters not that the earth may be moved, or the mountains may be lifted into the sea, or the great deep may boil, or that the land may quake and burst. It matters not, because in the midst of the turmoil there is one place that is tranquil. In the midst of the upheaval there is one place that is stable. In the midst of the faltering and flux there is one place which is unmoveable. In the midst of the shaking there is one place which is utterly unshakeable. And that one place is the City of God. It is unmoveable and utterly safe because in that city is the holy place, and in the holy place is the God of the elect.

The mountains may topple, the heathen may rage and the nations may roar, and it matters not. God is in His holy place, and He will be exalted. So in verse 10:

"Be still, and know that I am God: I will be exalted among the heathen, I will be exalted in the earth." Men who know this are called upon to be still and to know what their God is like. Notice too that the confidence just described is developed, and sharply focused in one sentence which occurs twice in the psalm, in verses 7 and 11: "The LORD of hosts is with us; the God of Jacob is our refuge." Here we are touching something that is quite central to the God-governed life, about the God who governs. First of all He is with us, and secondly He is our refuge. We must ponder that twofold declaration, for it epitomises the spirit of this psalm. So we shall focus sharply on that sentence, which is the central fact of the psalm: "Yahweh of hosts ... the God of Jacob."

A special and unique name

Readers will know that the name Yahweh is special and unique. It reveals the Deity as self-existent and eternal. Other names revealed in the Bible are sometimes preceded by qualifying words, but never so with this word, Yahweh. The Hebrews never wrote the Name fully: it was the incommunicable Name, which stood lonely and majestic as the sign and symbol of the deepest and the most intimate and infinite things about their God. It was to some extent inexplicable, in some sense incomprehensible – yet in some sense understandable. There is something about it that nobody can perfectly explain. It gives expression to those things about God that are the profoundest things of all: His absoluteness – without beginning, without end, without the taking of counsel, without forethought. For there was neither tongue, nor wisdom, nor counsel before Him. We have come to understand the Name also in this way: it represents the revelation of God manifestation. Through the teaching of earlier brethren we have come to understand that it reveals a God who is a continuous God, a God who will be continued in a sense in others – the becoming God, "I am who I am"; "I will be who I will be". He is a God becoming to others all that they need, revealing the self-determining power of the Most High, marking His utter sufficiency for all the needs of men and becoming to them all that they need in their sorrow, sadness and utter predicament. So we are in the presence of the greatest of all the words into which the fact of God has been compressed: "Yahweh of hosts".

"Yahweh of hosts"

As we look at Psalm 46 we ought to notice that the Psalmist came very near to qualifying this great Name, for he said "Yahweh of hosts". The words "of hosts" are not actually a qualification of Yahweh. The truth is that in a sense Yahweh qualifies the word "hosts", for they are His hosts. Let us look at this word "hosts", which is used in the Bible in differing ways. First of all, it is a word used and applied to stars. In Genesis 2:1 we read, "Thus the heavens and the earth were finished, and all the host of them." In Isaiah 40:26, "Lift up your eyes on high, and behold who hath created these things, that bringeth out their host by number: he calleth them all by names by the greatness of his might, for that he is strong in power; not one faileth." So "hosts" is applied to stars.

Next, "hosts" is applied to angels: "I saw the LORD sitting on his throne, and all the host of heaven standing by him on his right hand and on his left" (1 Kings 22:19). And in the song that was sounded over Bethlehem so long ago when earth was waiting, spent and restless: "Suddenly there was with the angel a multitude of the heavenly host praising God, and saying ..." (Luke 2:13). So hosts applies also to angels. Then there is something else. In Exodus the word "host" is applied to the children of Israel. They are called "the host" of God when in the wilderness (Exodus 16:13).

Bringing these thoughts together, notice that the word is used of stars in the heavens, of angels the ministers of God in heaven, beyond our vision and for the most part outside our knowledge, and then of companies of people who march across the earth and dwell upon its surface: stars and seraphim and saints; hosts of stars, hosts of angels, hosts of men.

With that in mind, return to that phrase in Psalm 46, "Yahweh of hosts". It tells us that God is superior to all these forces which are compressed into the word "hosts"; He is master of all those forces. He is the Lord of the hosts, whatever they are. He is pre-eminent and absolutely far and above all these things; He is their Lord. He is sufficient and superior to all these things in every way. He is the Lord of the heavens; He knows all the hosts of the heavens, and He marshals them at His will. But more, He is Lord of all the angelic hosts. In Psalm 103 we read, "Bless the LORD, ye his angels, that excel in strength, that do his commandments, hearkening unto the voice of his word" (Psalm 103:20).

Then He is the Lord of the world of men: He "ruleth in the kingdom of men, and giveth it to whomsoever he will" (Daniel 4:17). Every hair of every man and woman is numbered. Not a sparrow falls to the ground without His knowledge. The universe of matter, the universe of spirit, the universe of mind – He controls and marshals them all with infinite wisdom and unchallenged might. So in the phrase, "Yahweh of hosts" we are reminded of the absolute power and majesty and might and wisdom of the great God of heaven, Lord of the universe.

"The God of Jacob"

In other words, we are given a vision of one side of the great Creator, the sustainer of life here and everywhere, one side of His great majestic existence. But this is the thing to marvel at. In this short sentence suddenly we are given another view of the great God of heaven: "Yahweh of hosts ...", then quite suddenly, daringly, startlingly "... the God of Jacob". Just think where we were, amid the great cosmic conception of the invisible Creator. We were amid the eternal expanse of His great realm: the angels who can blind us with their light and glory, baffle us with their power. We were among the stellar spaces of the universe, and then quite suddenly, without warning, we move from that to this: "the God of Jacob".

The stars grow dim, and the angel hosts fade, and suddenly we are on one small planet in one small country looking into the face of one lonely man, Jacob the supplanter. We must understand that the Psalmist is telling us this for our salvation, that the God who is Lord of the universe, the God who is Lord of all the heavenly hosts, cosmic and angelic, the Creator of the stellar spaces, the Creator of the angelic intelligences – that great God is also the God of that speck of humanity, that lonely man called Jacob. Just as positively the great God is committed to that man as He is committed to all the order of His infinite universe. That is what we have to learn from that sentence.

In the Bible every word is important and it is no coincidence that the phrase is, "Yahweh of hosts is with us; the God of Jacob is our refuge". It is no coincidence that it is Jacob, the supplanter, Jacob the heel-catcher. What do you think about Jacob? There are varying views about him. Some think he was a hard mean man, self-sufficient and astute. But there was one man in the Bible who was harder, meaner and more self-sufficient, and that man was Laban. Of all the hard, astute, hard-driving mean men, I would think Laban is number one, but he met his match in Jacob.

Whatever you may think about Jacob, fix on this: whatever he was God cared for him, nurtured him, watched over him, kept His covenant with him. God defeated him at Jabbock and in the defeat made him to triumph, renamed him with a wonderful name: Israel, which means God-mastered, God-governed. That's the mystery, "the God of Jacob" – all through the years, in spite of the deception, notwithstanding whatever he did. In spite of his weakness, in spite of his self-assurance, God enwrapped him with His care, told him where to rest his head, gave him a vision of covenanted love at Bethel. And God cared for him when this Jacob was filled with fear as he left Paran to meet his brother

Esau, full of foreboding over what Esau would be feeling after forty years from the time of the deception, brooding about the way in which he had been deceived and supplanted. At last God made Esau's anger which Jacob feared to be turned into love, and instead of wrath the brothers greeted each other with a kiss.

This is the revelation: "Yahweh of hosts", infinite in majesty, stupendous in power; "the God of Jacob", infinite in mercy. "Yahweh of hosts", upholding all things by His commanding word, and then "the God of Jacob", sublime in His pity. Here is the wonder of it: when you think of the stellar spaces, when you think of the light years, the galaxies, when you think of the myriads of angels, the cherubim and the seraphim – "Yahweh of hosts" is wonderful, but it's so far away, and outside our experience. It is wonderful, but it is beyond us. The eternal order amid the stars and among the angels is awesome; it is distant. Just a glimpse of His glory on a starry night seems so far away.

This psalm tells us we are wrong: He is not far away. The Psalmist tells us, He is with Jacob, this infinite God of the stellar spaces. He is with Jacob, and because he is with Jacob He is also with us now. It is not only the immensity of the world the great God is revealed in, it's in the infinity of smallness sometimes that He is revealed as well. He is not far away, notwithstanding the failure, notwithstanding the inconstancy, despite the great gulf between what God intended and what man has done. In spite of the fact that life has been blighted and humanity ravaged by the dwarfing influences of sin, and notwithstanding man's selfishness, this Yahweh has created man and made him for one purpose only: to give glory to his Creator. And the creature has brought shame and degradation into the world, and broken all the holy laws which God has given, and ravaged His purpose. But still He is the God of Jacob. Still He broods over him, tenderly and carefully and tirelessly and lovingly, his folly notwithstanding.

With all this on our hearts, look at Psalm 46 again:

> "The LORD of hosts is with us; the God of Jacob is our refuge."

The God of the stars, and of the angels, the God of many multitudes, is with us for the making of Jacob, and therefore for the making of all others who share Jacob's faith. The wonderful teaching of this psalm is that God will press all these hosts, over which He reigns, into that service and for that purpose, if it be necessary. The God who controls these hosts will control them for our sakes, and for Jacob's sake, because he is "our refuge".

"The stars in their courses"

Now you may feel that is a very far-fetched idea. Could it mean that God would use the stars for the making and re-making of those who are destined for high purpose in the great plan of redemption? Recollect something written in the Song of Deborah, the Bible's angry young woman:

> "Gilead abode beyond Jordan: and why did Dan remain in ships? Asher continued on the sea shore, and abode in his breaches. Zebulun and Naphtali were a people that jeoparded their lives unto the death in the high places of the field. The kings came and fought, then fought the kings of Canaan in Taanach by the waters of Megiddo; they took no gain of money. They fought from heaven; the stars in their courses fought against Sisera. The river of Kishon swept them away, that ancient river, the river Kishon. O my soul, thou hast trodden down strength. Then were the horsehoofs broken by the means of the pransings, the pransings of their mighty ones. Curse ye Meroz, said the angel of the LORD, curse ye bitterly the inhabitants thereof; because they came not to the help of the LORD, to the help of the LORD against the mighty." (Judges 5:17-23)

You will notice in this song that Deborah deplores the fact that there were some who did nothing to advance the cause of God, and God's people: Dan remained in his ships, Asher sat still, others arrested themselves by the watercourses of Reuben, ruminating and talking and doing nothing. But notwithstanding, there were forces in heaven that fought for the chosen of the Lord. And what were the forces? The stars! "The stars in their courses fought against Sisera". You will be asking, what does it mean? "The stars in their courses fought ..." Possibly what happened was this: just as the River Nile floods, when Sirius the dogstar rises, so perhaps the River Kishon flooded by the influence of the stars.

Now this is what happened in fact: "The river of Kishon swept them away." The flooded river carried them away. It is so much a reality, so much a wonderful fact, that you will notice Deborah stops telling the account of what happened in order to exclaim, "O my soul, march on with strength" (verse 21, RV). Deborah is so moved by the realisation and recollection of what happened and the wonder of it. So the Lord has at least once commanded the stars and used them in the course of His great purpose. Dare we say He will never do it again?

Think of this: once He counted the life of the Lord of the stars worth giving for the saving of broken humanity. Once the balances were held up, and a voice said: "For what shall a man be profited, if he shall gain the whole world, and forfeit his life? or what shall a man give in exchange for his life?" (Matthew 16:26, RV). If He shall give the one for whom the stars have been created, and the one in whom the very stars consist, if He will give him for the sake of saving man, He surely will not hesitate to use the stars in that purpose if they were needed.

"Ministering spirits"

Need the premise be argued in the case of angels? Will He use the angels? "The angel of the LORD encampeth round about them that fear him, and delivereth them" (Psalm 34:7). "Are they not all ministering spirits, sent forth to minister for them who shall be heirs of salvation?" (Hebrews 1:14). "Take heed that ye despise not one of these little ones; for I say unto you, That in heaven their angels do always behold the face of my Father which is in heaven" (Matthew 18:10). What is the great word that once fell from the lips of the King himself: "Thinkest thou that I cannot now pray to my Father, and he shall presently give me more than twelve legions of angels?" (Matthew 26:53). Remember once, God responding to the word of Elijah the prophet opened the eyes of that fearful man who was with him, and the man saw the mountain full of angels and flaming with angel light. The premise does not need arguing: it is too evident.

The hosts of men

What about the hosts of men? Will He use those in His great purpose to save us? Well, He is Lord of all the hosts of men, of all the armies in the world. If men will fight, and they will, we can be sure that He is the God of battles, El Gibbor. He rules in the kingdoms of men, and sets up whomsoever He will, and when men make war, He governs their goings. No army ever marches across the face of the earth but it is under the control of His strong hand.

Now this is the truth: He will compel the march of men to the making of His own men, and in the fulfilling of His great purpose. Think of Ezekiel 38, the armies of Gog, how are they moving? By their own volition altogether? "I will ... put hooks into thy jaws", said the voice (Ezekiel 38:4). He is Lord of all: Lord of the physicist, Lord of the architect, Lord of the scientist. In a way, they discover what He is disposed to reveal, at the time of His choosing. Every discovery of man may be a revelation from God. It is surely no coincidence that when in the purpose of God it came time for the great spiritual reformation in Europe which would result in the unveiling of the Truth in the latter days, that men discovered printing. It is no coincidence that, as the world moves towards its final hour of agony, men have discovered nuclear fission.

Carlyle once said, "God may be in His heaven, but He does nothing". Carlyle was wrong: God is in His heaven and is always doing something. He is the Lord of hosts, and will press into His service for the making of Jacob into Israel, the host of stars, the host of angels and the hosts of men. Of that we can be sure.

Our refuge

What must be examined finally is this: What does it mean, "The God of Jacob is our refuge"? We need to discover in what way God was a refuge to Jacob. Recollect how patiently and painstakingly God worked upon Jacob. Think what He did to recover this lonely man for Himself. He opened the heavens and He fixed the ladder, and on the ladder the ascending and descending angels. One day He gave him a vision of hosts, and Jacob called the place Mahanaim, which means 'the place of two hosts'. And Jacob said, "With my staff I passed over this Jordan; and now I am become two companies" (Genesis 32:10, RV). It's a strange phrase, suggesting that Jacob was rejoicing about how his possessions had multiplied since he first crossed Jordan. He had doubled his possessions and he had to learn that none of them were really His own. The Lord of hosts is Lord over Jacob's possessions. He is the Lord of Jacob's hosts, possessing every last skin of beast, and every last shekel.

Then there were the hosts of Esau. Esau was coming, and you will notice it says he was coming with a host of men to meet Jacob. And then Jacob met God at Peniel and was crippled. There was a strange night of wrestling with God, and as a result Jacob was crippled. He was never the same again; he was a limping man, "him that halteth". But the mystery is that in the crippling he was made whole; in the breaking he was healed. Jacob said to the man of God, "I will not let thee go, except thou bless me" (Genesis 32:26). If only we knew how he said it, we should know a lot more about this mysterious situation. If only we knew the tone of voice. Did he say it stridently, strongly, demandingly, like it sounds? The tone of voice can make a world of difference. There are two ways of saying, "I love you", and one is better than the other.

Here's a strange thing, a wonderful thing, for hundreds of years afterwards a prophet, speaking about something entirely different, let slip the tone of Jacob's voice:

> "The LORD hath also a controversy with Judah, and will punish Jacob according to his ways; according to his doings will he recompense him. He took his brother by the heel in the womb, and by his strength he had power with God: yea, he had power over the angel, and prevailed: he wept, and made supplication unto him: he found him in Bethel, and there he spake with us; even the LORD God of hosts; the LORD is his memorial." (Hosea 12:2-5)

"He wept, and made supplication ..." There is the revelation. It was not spoken stridently at all. It was a voice choked with tears; it was the last sob of a defeated man, going down in the final agony of despair beneath the pressure of the mysterious man of God. This is the mystery: he triumphed in the moment he was beaten, he was remade when he was broken, he was made whole when he was crippled. A man cannot defeat God; nobody defeats God. A man comes to victory with God when God defeats him. That's the truth of it. What a man yields to God, he wins. It is the absolute opposite of the principle of normal life. That is why his name is Israel: it tells of his new status. It means God-mastered – not Jacob mastering God, but God mastering him.

You may say, Israel means 'Prince with God', but it does so only inferentially, in the sense that a man has power with God when that man is defeated by God. Then he becomes a prince. A man is exalted to be a prince when he is humbled and submits. This is the great principle of the New Testament, and it is what Jacob experienced. Imagine him limping up from the brook at Jabbock to his friends who have been waiting all the night wondering what has happened to him. He limps up to them and tells them he is no more Jacob the supplanter, but Israel, God-governed – mastered by God so that he may have power with God.

This is what happened to him, and somewhere in this experience is the idea of "refuge". The inference of the Psalmist's words is that not only is God our refuge, but that He was a refuge for Jacob as well. Some will understand this – those with long experience of life, and on whom God has put His hand. They have been wounded and discovered that in the very wounding can be found His healing. They have been crippled perhaps, and mysteriously in the very crippling have been made strong for more service. It's mysterious. Cherished dreams perhaps have been shattered, but in such a way that the visions of deeper things have been realised and followed. It may be they would say they will never be the same again. But ask them if they would be different, if they would be without it. Ask them if in the passing through Peniel they would have wished to retrace their steps and miss it – and they will say they wouldn't be without it.

The God of Jacob is their refuge. The Lord of hosts is marshalling the forces to make whole those who are broken. This word "refuge" is interesting – its first meaning is 'the high place'. "The name of the LORD is a strong tower: the righteous runneth into it, and is safe" (Proverbs 18:10). Here is the idea of refuge in a tower; in the high place men can be set above the circumstances, above the forces that hurt or harm, above the enemies, above self. They can rise above the things that hinder and impede, and fetter and degrade. Therefore they look to the future with confidence, from the high place, from the refuge and security, because "The LORD of hosts is with us; the God of Jacob is our refuge".

How, if we can put our faith in this assurance, will it affect us? What will be, could be, or should be the result of this realisation upon our daily lives – the daily manifestation of the God-governed life? The proposition is that it ought to be seen in the quiet calm of our spirit, in the tenderness of our compassion, in the straightness of our dealings, and in the developing faithfulness of our living. As you ponder it, and seek to appropriate it according to your faith, it will happen in proportion to your yielding to the word that is written, which is a light in a dark world; it will happen in proportion to the will that is known and understood – the will of God; to the service which is discovered in the needs of God's people. And so we may know that the Lord of hosts is with us: the Lord of order and precision, the Lord of power; and the God of Jacob: the God of love and care and sympathy.

"The LORD of hosts is with us; the God of Jacob is our refuge."

This is at the very centre of the God-governed life. May God grant that all may realise it and feel it to be true in the oncoming days.

4

ALL THINGS WORK TOGETHER FOR GOOD
PSALM 77

YOU will notice that Psalm 77 was composed by a man named Asaph, and here are a few details about him. He lived at the same time as King David, and was a member of David's court: a person of importance and influence. He was a musician, and a very accomplished songwriter appointed by the king to be the chief choirmaster for the services of worship and praise. There were about four thousand musicians of which 288 were well-practised and very skilful. The remainder were assistants and pupils. There were three principal conductors, Asaph, Heman and Ethan. Asaph was the chief.

As to his personal details: he was a Levite; his father's name was Berechiah, and he composed among others Psalms 73-83. Music almost certainly ran in the family, and perhaps the high honour of being singers and musicians for God in the worship of the brotherhood of Israel was an hereditary honour, handed down from father to son. But Asaph was more than a great musician. He was also a prophet – else why could his songs be included in the great book of the inspired Psalms of Israel? In 2 Chronicles 29:30 Asaph is equated with David the prophet and nominated as a "seer" of Israel.

These are the personal details found in the Bible narrative, but there is something more to be learned about him in Psalm 77 which is not found in the historical records. If you have ever looked through a telescope or binoculars, you may have found the vision blurred, uncertain, indistinct, dislocated, or misty. By making necessary adjustments, suddenly the mists are cleared, the picture is defined, the lines are sharp, the uncertainty is gone, everything is in perspective and in true focus. Something like this happened to Asaph, not when looking through a telescope, but when he was looking at life. His experience, and how he found it, are recorded in Psalm 77 – the story of Asaph looking at life. How did he see it?

A song of perplexity and grief

Look carefully at the first nine verses. It is a sad, sobbing song of perplexity and grief. It is full of complaint, heavy with agony and there is no comfort. His life seems to be a perpetual mystery. Nothing seems right, everything is dislocated. His words come tumbling out, for there are so many personal problems – and so many personal pronouns. It is full of adversity. In the first ten verses you will find eleven references to God and twenty-two personal references to Asaph. This is not a criticism, but it marks the condition of his soul. He is full of trouble and resolves to cry to God in his anguish and despair. Notice his words:

> "I will cry unto God with my voice; even unto God with my voice, and he will give ear unto me."
>
> (Psalm 77:1, RV)

But there was no comfort and no healing:

> "In the day of my trouble I sought the Lord: my sore ran in the night, and ceased not: my soul refused to be comforted. I remembered God, and was troubled: I complained, and my spirit was overwhelmed." (verses 2,3)

So, remembering God brought him no peace. He complained, but that brought him no comfort.

> "Thou holdest mine eyes waking: I am so troubled that I cannot speak." (verse 4)

Even his insomnia he blames on God. And then he tries to get comfort by bringing to mind his past experience. He thinks that if he can recapture the joy he had then, it will bring him solace. But it does no good:

> "I have considered the days of old, the years of ancient times. I call to remembrance my song in the night." (verses 5,6)

But although he calls it to remembrance, the old joy that it then generated doesn't return now. His perplexity is too real, and his adversity too present to be alleviated by remembering past happiness. So at last there stumble from his heart and lips questions of doubt and despair:

> "Will the Lord cast off for ever? and will he be favourable no more? Is his mercy clean gone for ever? doth his promise fail for evermore? Hath God forgotten to be gracious? hath he in anger shut up his tender mercies?" (verses 7-9)

We can see the dark desolation that descended upon his despairing soul. That was the vision he saw as he looked at life. Nothing was right, everything was dislocated, the picture was uncertain, the definition was clouded; all of it was out of focus. That was his view of life as it is revealed to us in the first nine verses of this psalm.

Hope and encouragement

But here is a startling thing. Mark his view of the very same life in the last nine verses. Remember it is the same picture, but how differently he sees it. The man who in verse 9 asked, "Hath God forgotten to be gracious?" is now saying:

> "Thy way, O God, is in the sanctuary: who is so great a God as our God? Thou art the God that doest wonders: thou hast declared thy strength among the people. Thou hast with thine arm redeemed thy people." (verses 13-15)

The man who previously was full of despair and desolation in the midst of his perplexing life is now in the midst of the very same life, but full of hope and encouragement. It seems that he is marching now with his head held high. He is singing a song of redemption and deliverance. In spite of the same opposition, and notwithstanding the same circumstances, he is marching on to victory – and he is singing! He sings, not because the adversity has ceased, not because the hostility is over or the opposition is gone; he is singing because for some reason these things do not matter as they once did. For some reason he has found the true focus.

What is the explanation? Suddenly, everything is well. What happened to Asaph to change his vision of life from darkness to light – from one who had nearly lost his hold on God to one who will not let go, come what may? What happened?

We have to be honest, and say that we do not know. But whatever it was, we must believe that it came from God. To illustrate this, look at Psalm 73 – another of Asaph's psalms:

> "Truly God is good to Israel, even to such as are of a clean heart. But as for me, my feet were almost gone; my steps had well nigh slipped."
>
> (Psalm 73:1,2)

This must be the same thing as in Psalm 77. Asaph says that his "steps had well nigh slipped". Now look later in the same Psalm:

> "... my feet were almost gone; my steps had well nigh slipped ... Until I went into the sanctuary of God; then understood I their end." (verses 2,17)

The result was that Asaph saw and understood something which hitherto he had missed. There was a realisation of something which, in his despair he had not grasped. As though in a moment, suddenly, he made the adjustment and the vision, the cloudy vision, came into focus. Whatever it was he saw, it's in Psalm 77:10. Look at that verse carefully, and leave out the words in italics ("but I will remember"). These were added by the translators to give the sense they thought should be there, but in this instance they may not help us:

> "And I said, This is my infirmity ... the years of the right hand of the most High." (Psalm 77:10)

Whatever that means, it puts the picture into focus. Consider this proposal, that the years referred to in verse 10, "the years of the right hand of the most High" are the years of Asaph's life, and not the years of God's life, for His existence is outside human time. The Psalmist is therefore speaking here of his own years, measured in his mind and known in his own experience. What he is saying is that his infirmity and the perplexing years of his life, so full of adversity and mystery, have really belonged to God all the time, and have been always in the power of His right hand. What he thought to be years of mischance have been years that were, through the strange circumstances of life, moulded, conditioned, guided and fashioned by the right hand of God: "This is my infirmity ... the years of the right hand of the most High".

All the time he seemed to be alone and bereft, God knew it and it was part of His pattern, made within His purpose, encompassed by His law and His righteousness. All those years, those perplexing years when it seemed that poor Asaph was well nigh lost, in spite of his eminence, status and high calling, God had been working in him, willing and doing of His good pleasure. All through the adversity he was being caressed by the love of God. The pressure of the potter on the wheel, sometimes hard, sometimes gentle, was always with the view of making at last a vessel beautiful and worthy of its high destiny. The strange years were held within the right hand of the most High, and what Asaph realised at last was a forecast of the great New Testament words, "All things work together for good to them that love God, to them who are the called according to his purpose" (Romans 8:28).

"The right hand of the most High"

This was the adjustment that brought this man's life into true focus. To penetrate further into the mind of this man Asaph, we must ask what the right hand of God would mean to him as a devout Hebrew. Think of how the term is used in the Hebrew scriptures:

"From his (God's) right hand went a fiery law for them (the children of Israel)." (Deuteronomy 33:2)

"O God, so is thy praise unto the ends of the earth: thy right hand is full of righteousness." (Psalm 48:10)

"Shew thy marvellous lovingkindness, O thou that savest by thy right hand them which put their trust in thee from those that rise up against them." (17:7)

"Now know I that the LORD saveth his anointed; he will hear him from his holy heaven with the saving strength of his right hand." (20:6)

"The right hand of the LORD is exalted: the right hand of the LORD doeth valiantly." (118:16)

"His left hand is under my head, and his right hand doth embrace me." (Song of Solomon 2:6)

"In thy presence is fulness of joy; at thy right hand there are pleasures for evermore." (Psalm 16:11)

From this brief review we can grasp how a devout Hebrew would understand the right hand of God, and perhaps those ideas would be in the mind of Asaph, well-versed in the revelation of God's word. Putting all the ideas together, it would mean the vision of his life encompassed by divine authority, related to God's salvation, sustained by His strength, guided by His activity, mastered by His love, and at last fully satisfied by participating in the joy of God's glorious purpose. This was the true focus. No wonder it turned darkness into light, and the despairing desolation into a great doxology.

The majesty and power of God

There is something else that ought not to surprise us. In the latter verses of his song in Psalm 77, Asaph expresses his relief and satisfaction in terms of the majesty and the power of God, using figures of great waters, thunder and lightning. So often when men of God are in despair and desolation, God revives them by deepening their consciousness of His majesty, His greatness and His power. It was so with Job. When he was at his deepest desolation, and when we should have been offering some soothing word of comfort, if we had been there, God gave him a vision of His own majesty and glory. As a result of seeing God in that way the soul of Job was healed. And so it was with Isaiah at the time the king died and the prophet faced trial and difficulty. He said:

> "I saw also the Lord sitting upon a throne, high and lifted up, and his train filled the temple."
>
> (Isaiah 6:1)

It was the same for Ezekiel, as an exile lonely by the River Chebar: there he saw a great vision of glory, a mysterious vision, and he was sustained by it. With Elijah too, when he wished to die for despair, God gave him a great vision in the mountain. And so it was with the man of Nazareth, just as he turned to make his last bitter journey to the cross-crowned hill, on the mountain where Elijah had stood, he stood again with Moses and with Jesus and God deepened His Son's consciousness of the glory that would follow. He saw of the travail of his soul, and was satisfied.

Let us not be surprised if Asaph, seeing life in its true focus, tells out the greatness and the healing glory of God. In a deepening consciousness of God's greatness and His purpose, this man loses his consciousness of his own infirmity. It is swallowed up by a deepening awareness of the glory of God. A little analysis will prove this to be true. In the last nine verses of Psalm 77, Asaph is mentioned three times and God is mentioned twenty-four times. The forces which are mighty and majestic in vision are gentle and healing in their therapeutic effect upon the soul. It's like the Sun, the most powerful force in our experience, but notwithstanding its unimaginable power, how gently it brings the primrose to its fulfilment and with what tenderness it brings the rose to its glory.

A great Shepherd

This is the story of Asaph. It began, "I will cry unto God with my voice"; it ends, "Thou leddest thy people like a flock". The cry for help was answered at last by a realisation of what God is like, and the revelation to Asaph was that God is a great shepherd. We know that was a story of a long time ago, but consider that it is also the story of yesterday. How have we arrived at the current stage in our lives? Sometimes life and our vision of it is misty and dislocated and uncertain. Sometimes we ask the questions which fell from the lips of Asaph. Sometimes we hide away in perplexity, bruised or bewildered, sighing because burdened with some weakness, sorrowed by some failure, or disappointed by the development of life.

On the authority of Asaph's testimony, let us not hide our questions and problems from God, because He dealt with Asaph. And if He can deal with Asaph, He can deal with us and can guide us to the same solution: that the right hand of God is there and active. Looking back in retrospection we can see the hand of God, and are able to say, 'Yes, that was one of the years of the right hand of the most High. It was part of His fiery law; it was hard, but now I know it was part of the ministry of divine love. It had the promise of joy in it for evermore, even though at the time it seemed grievous'.

Like Jacob you will be able to say, "Surely, God was in this place, and I knew it not" – the nearness of God, unrecognised but at last discovered. So the mists clear, the vision is defined, the understanding is illuminated, and we come nearer to the true focus. Perchance we may be able to say with Asaph:

> "Thou art the God that doest wonders: thou hast declared thy strength among the people. Thou hast with thine arm redeemed thy people."
>
> (Psalm 77:14,15)

Here is something to give us confidence. When you read the Gospel narrative of the Son of God walking the streets and hills of Galilee, you are aware that men saw in him the fact that God cared immeasurably, superlatively for His people. His interest in them was not just theoretic and academic; it was real and practical. Through Jesus of Nazareth, people became aware that the Father was sensitive to the human predicament. He made a man stand upright who had lain for thirty-eight withered, wintry years at Bethesda; He felt all the agony of the widow of Nain, whose only boy lay dead upon the bier; He felt the dull, paralysing pain of the two sisters at Bethany when they lost their brother. Men and women saw and knew that God cared about their sorrow, about their sobbing, about their sadness. They saw through this man of Nazareth that God is a great Shepherd.

"All things work together for good ..."

We sometimes speak of accidents and catastrophes, and it's right that we should, for all are subject to the laws of the universe. Whatever happens to us, happens to other men, but it happens to us in the realm of God's purpose. It happens to us with His knowledge and in the orbit of His will, for "all things work together for good to them that love God, to them who are the called according to his purpose" (Romans 8:28). Some have interpreted that sentence in this way. They put their idea into a very attractive proposition, by taking that sentence to mean that God tempers the wind to the shorn lamb: He rearranges the forces and events of the world to shield His children from the hard effects of life. It is to be doubted that this is the principle on which God deals with His children. He does not alter the eternal laws of the universe to suit the particular circumstances of an individual life; He does not temper the wind to the shorn lamb.

But what God does is to leave the wind as it is, and give the lamb a good thick coat to stand against it! Or He so uses the force of the wind that, however it works, in the end the lamb is stronger and better than at the beginning of the experience. And whatever is permitted, be it ever so perplexing, is permitted so that ultimately it may save and do good, and never do harm and destroy. Why is that? On the authority of the great Apostle Peter and by the ministration of the Holy Spirit, "He careth for you" (1 Peter 5:7).

"In all thy ways acknowledge him"

Either that is true, or there is some part of the Bible which is false. In our deepest heart, we believe it to be true because His covenant is ordered in all things and sure, and our infirmities can be in the right hand of the most High: "In all thy ways acknowledge him, and he shall direct thy paths" (Proverbs 3:6). This means, see Him everywhere, in all the varied ways of life, like Jesus did. In the commonplace things of life, Jesus saw his Father. He saw the flowers and said, God clothes them. He heard the birds singing, and said, "Your Heavenly Father feedeth them". He handled a common loaf, and said, there is bread that men may eat and not taste of death for ever. He saw the shepherd on the hillside and said, the shepherd work of God will never cease.

See God everywhere, and He shall direct your paths. That is the true focus. So come back to the point about the way in which all things work together for good. God does not alter the eternal laws of the universe in order to protect His children; He does not usually temper the wind to the shorn lamb. The change is not necessarily in the circumstances of life; usually it is in our attitude to them. Mystery deepened intensifies our fear; mystery resolved relieves and removes it. The circumstances do not change, but because we understand them better, the terror, worry and anxiety are removed.

Those men on the sea who saw a phantom, a spirit, an apparition, were terrified. And out of the apparition a voice spoke, "Be of good cheer; it is I; be not afraid". Immediately, their attitude changed and their fear disappeared. Their misunderstanding had turned their Lord into a phantom, but when they recognised him, their fear went. The circumstances hadn't changed, but their attitude had. This is a very important principle, and another good example is to be found in Philippians:

> "Not that I speak in respect of want: for I have learned, in whatsoever state I am, therewith to be

> content. I know both how to be abased, and I know how to abound: every where and in all things I am instructed both to be full and to be hungry, both to abound and to suffer need." (Philippians 4:11,12)

Whether the circumstances were bountiful or meagre, the Apostle Paul had learned to live with either condition happily. In other words, it was mastery by detachment. He was thankful for enough, and he wasn't miserable and dismayed when there was a shortage. He was able to live under both conditions, and it was his right attitude to both that enabled him to be mastered by neither. In that sense, he was able to detach himself successfully from the circumstances. He had learned the lesson: circumstances may remain the same, but it is our attitude to them that makes all the difference.

This is the lesson Asaph learned. The laws of the universe are immutable. God uses them, not changes them, for our good. In the end, it's our attitude that determines whether we master them or they master us. This could well be the secret of right praying: not that God will temper the wind, but that we may be strengthened to stand against it; not that the laws might be changed, but that we may be able to use them rightly or wisely.

Come back to the proverb:

> "In all thy ways acknowledge him, and he shall direct thy paths." (Proverbs 3:6)

This is an important statement in the light of Psalm 77. What we have to face is that although God directs our paths, He does so in strange ways, and not the ways we would choose: perplexing ways, baffling ways. He does not always do what we want. Sometimes people have lived to thank God that He did not answer their prayers as they wanted. In retrospection they realise that, had He done so, it would have brought disaster. People have lived to thank God that He refused their most cherished ambitions, and He did it for love's sake. The way things "work together for good" are sometimes very strange indeed. Here, he puts an obstacle in the way; there He removes one. Today He flings us out into new circumstances; tomorrow He keeps us at home. Today He disappoints us; tomorrow He fulfils our dreams. There are things to be learned, truths to be realised, influences to be received and to be rejected. God uses the events and the circumstances of our lives, the joys and infirmities, to make things work together for good.

Think what it means, perhaps, in the intricacies of some present problem, the agony of some deep sorrow, the hush of some momentous decision that has to be faced and taken, the commonplace matters of daily life: all these things are in the realm of His caring activity. It is false to say that God works in the sanctuary but never in the market place. Acknowledge God in all thy ways, and He shall direct thy paths. In the God-governed life, while the circumstances of life do not usually change, what changes is God's influence and our attitude towards them.

"The just shall live by his faith"

This was so in Asaph's life, and a very good example of the same principle operated in the life of another prophet, Habakkuk. He had a problem. Everything was going wrong, and he was perplexed by God's apparent indifference. The Chaldeans were ravaging the land and spoiling and violence were everywhere. The law was despised, judgement was abandoned. The wicked were in the place of power, and contention was rife. As Habakkuk saw it, God did nothing. When a young man, I used to go on walks with an older brother, and we talked about the Bible. One day he said, "Do you know, Habakkuk shook his fist at God?" This seemed very shocking, but I now understand it better. 'How long?' Habakkuk said, 'I cry day and night, I cry of violence, and you do nothing'.

Poor Habakkuk was perplexed and desolate, and waited to see what God would say to him in his despair. God spoke to him when he was in the tower and said, 'Habakkuk, I am not indifferent. I am at work. But if I told you what I was doing, you would hardly believe me.

This is the mystery for you, Habakkuk. I am employing the Chaldeans, people who are outside the covenant, as my instruments to punish my people for their wickedness'.

Habakkuk was staggered: how can you employ men more wicked than they in order to punish them? God declared to him the principle of all true life. The puffed up soul will be destroyed, but the righteous soul must live by faith. The Chaldeans in their pride and arrogant wickedness would be destroyed, but those like Habakkuk must trust in God and have faith. Habakkuk's reply was to all intents and purposes this: 'Yahweh, I thought you had forsaken us, but now I know you are working for the salvation of your people. I am still perplexed, O Lord, but keep alive the work. Although I do not fully understand the method, and although just now I cannot fathom the secret, in the midst of the years make it known. Only in the day of your wrath, remember mercy.' And God said, "the just shall live by his faith".

Rejoicing in the Lord

Immediately the word was spoken, it was Asaph's case all over again. He believed it, he rested, and trustingly he rested on God. He was at peace. There was no change in the conditions; no amelioration of circumstances – the desolation was still imminent. Habakkuk's attitude was utterly changed. In the face of the very same things his life suddenly was readjusted and in perfect confidence and focus. He said, "I will rejoice in the LORD, I will joy in the God of my salvation". This means, I will jump for joy, I will dance for joy.

Notice in Habakkuk 3 the circumstances in which he made this declaration:

> "Although the fig tree shall not blossom, neither shall fruit be in the vines; the labour of the olive shall fail, and the fields shall yield no meat; the flock shall be cut off from the fold, and there shall be no herd in

> the stalls: yet I will rejoice in the LORD, I will joy in the God of my salvation." (Habakkuk 3:17,18)

In that verse 17 could there be a more desolate description of disaster? There is not one good thing mentioned. Fruit failing, labour ending, fields barren, flocks decimated, the herds gone. For an agricultural nation that is the most desolate description of life there is in the Bible. And the man says after showing it, "I will rejoice in the LORD"! A condition of utter disaster, but the prophet understood it by faith and was content.

This is precisely Asaph's experience repeated in the life of Habakkuk: the experience of the God-governed life. Out of the mystery of intricate patterns, perplexing failures, and contradictory experiences, the order of developing goodness emerges bit by bit. Imperceptibly, the right hand of God is discovered. All the topsy-turvy, aimless ways have been in His right hand all along. All the seeming indifference was really full of inspired activity. "Surely God was in this place, and we knew it not".

So let us renew our faith as did Asaph and Habakkuk – in spite of bruises, wounds, disappointments, doubts and perplexities. Let us look once more with enduring and wonderful faith on what God has done in the past, what He is doing now in the present, and what He will do ere long, magnificently. And let us say with tranquil trust, "Who is so great a God as our God? ... Thou hast with thine arm redeemed thy people ... Thou leddest thy people like a flock." God grant that you may feel it to be true.

5

THE UPRIGHT SHALL DWELL IN THY PRESENCE PSALM 140 / PSALM 16

THE title of this chapter is taken from Psalm 140, but is best developed in Psalm 16. By way of illustration first consider the last verse of Psalm 140: “Surely the righteous shall give thanks unto thy name: the upright shall dwell in thy presence”. This is the central idea of this chapter. The short sentence expresses all the promise of God for His people; all the aspirations of His people for divine fulfilment. On one hand are the upright, and on the other the presence of the great God. The two are merged in such a way that there is fulness of joy realised. For the upright – and for God Himself – fulness of joy is realised.

Now think of the words, “in thy presence”, and consider Psalm 16:11:

> “Thou wilt shew me the path of life: in thy presence is fulness of joy; at thy right hand there are pleasures for evermore.”

I affirm that the path of life is the path of the God-governed life, out of which will come fulness of joy and pleasures for evermore.

Our aim then is to consider that wonderful last verse of Psalm 140 as it is illuminated by Psalm 16.

But first, two points of exposition. We know on the authority of the Apostle Peter that these sentences towards the end of Psalm 16 were inscribed by the Holy Spirit about the King himself:

> “Thou wilt not leave my soul in hell; neither wilt thou suffer thine Holy One to see corruption.”
>
> (Psalms 16:10, cp. Acts 2:30,31)

Yet we must also agree that there is some application of the words at the end of Psalm 16 to the saints, especially in the last verse. That is permissible, for the King once said, "because I live, ye shall live also" (John 14:19). Paul said, "If we suffer (with him), we shall also reign with him" (2 Timothy 2:12). In Ephesians it is explained that, in prospect, the saints have been raised from the dead already in Christ Jesus.

It means that some of the words which have been written about the beloved Son of God are also true of God's other children. It means that what is true of the King is true also of those who have given him their allegiance. We are therefore reasonably safe to ponder these words in their possible application to ourselves, to some extent.

We do not know the interpretation that will be placed on that verse in Psalm 16, for in the strict chronological context of the psalm the words describe a post-resurrectional experience of the Son of God. But are we therefore to conclude that the words have no meaning for the saints until after their resurrection? As these words in the psalm occur after the resurrection of the Son ("Thou wilt not leave my soul in hell; neither wilt thou suffer thine Holy One to see corruption" precedes the comment about "the path of life"), does that mean that when they are applied to the saints the words only describe their post-resurrectional experience?

Is there no joy or pleasure until the corruptible body which we bear is made incorruptible? Is not the balanced interpretation in the context of Psalm 16 that these things were magnificently true after the Lord broke down the doors of the cold tomb and came out to life unsullied and unwearied, but also that the very principles on which they are based are perpetually true, and thus in a sense timeless? Is it not perpetually true that in the presence of God there is always joy? And is it not timelessly true that at His right hand there are pleasures for evermore, and that those who seek them sincerely and rightly may find them? So is it possible to accept that the words may have meaning for the life that now is, as well as for the life that is to come?

It must be evident that the words, "at thy right hand there are pleasures for evermore" provide a restatement of the phrase, "fulness of joy". In other words, one parallels the other.

"In thy presence"

Think first of all what is meant by being in the presence of God: "In thy presence is fulness of joy" – this is an essential part of the God-governed life. It is not good enough to say that because somebody has come to know the truth about God's purpose, they are therefore in His presence. It is certainly the case that no one can come into His presence without a knowledge of the truth, but in itself that is not a guarantee they are therefore in God's presence. It is not axiomatic that the presence of God's word, and the presence of God are the same thing. For example, you could say a man has the truth. But the truth is only really true for someone when it passes into action. To have it and to speculate upon it, and never to do it, you are not really in it. You have passed out of it, and therefore have passed out of the presence of God.

Think what causes a person to be outside the presence of God in a spiritual sense: to talk of another life, and then to live this life as though it were the only life; to talk of God, and then live as though He didn't exist; to see the material world, and never look through it to the spiritual world. It is a condition where the truth becomes a mask, worn sadly to hide the empty life and the lost passion. A man in the presence of God is a man using this life thankfully, rejoicingly, but always looking through it to the spiritual; a man who tries always to put the measurement of the infinite on transient things; a man who weighs this life's forces in the balance of eternity; a man who worships the Creator and never the creature; a man who being aware of the presence of God in the things of natural life, is by that token constantly in the divine presence.

This is to state the ideal, of course. Such a man was the King himself. He was man standing in the midst of the material world and seeing God everywhere: looking at flowers and saying, God clothes them; he heard the birds singing, and said, Your Father cares for them; he handled a common loaf, and spoke of the bread that leads to eternal life; he saw the vine growing in the field, and said it was but a replica of the true vine which will be given for the life of men; he looked at the shepherd on the hillside, and said God's shepherding work will go on until all the lambs are folded. He loved children and said, "their angels do always behold the face of my Father which is in heaven" (Matthew 18:10).

In the presence of commonplace things, he was at the same time in the presence of God because looking through them, he saw God everywhere. He stood on the plains of Judaea, his feet firmly on the earth, and then spoke of being in the bosom of the Father. Now, by contrast, those men who engineered his downfall were men knowing the purpose of God, men who sat in Moses' seat, men who handled the word of Israel's God every day. And yet they were outside His presence. They recited the creed every day and they were blind to the truth. They had so misunderstood the Lord of the universe that they thought He cared more for a clean plate than a clean heart. They made incidental things essential and became deaf to the voice of God. They never heard the music of the infinite. They never saw the life of light, and consequently they never came into the presence of God. It is written of one of them, he "prayed ... with himself" (Luke 18:11): the lonely isolation of a man who was never able to break the barrier and enter into God's presence.

"Fulness of joy"

Such a life is a joyless life. But the life that looks through the world to the spiritual is a life of joy in the real sense. Just pause to consider what joy really is. Joy is not cheerfulness. I'm not against cheerfulness, please don't think that, for cheerfulness is quite splendid. If one man comes to me to complain, and another to cheer me, I know which I prefer to see! But cheerfulness is different from joy. Cheerfulness, or human happiness depends on outward circumstances for its existence. If circumstances are congenial, then happiness exists. Human happiness is circumstantial; but joy is different.

Joy can exist when the circumstances are such as to make cheerfulness not only impossible, but inappropriate. We have an example of this in Acts 16 where two men are in prison in Philippi: their feet in the stocks, their backs torn by scourging, they are suffering excruciating pain. It is midnight, they are in the dark – and they are singing! They are singing the song of resurrection. They are not singing because they are comfortable, but because they have discovered a joy which transcends their pain. They care not for the darkness at all because they are citizens of that city where there is no night.

This is the path of life, and those men evidently had found it. They passed through the wicket gate into the path of life. Being in the presence of God even in the midst of their pain, they found joy – joy enough to sing. So the term "fulness of joy" means that no department of life is excluded. Note that it does not just talk of "joy" but the "fulness of joy": nothing excluded from it, every part enriched, every activity ennobled, every endeavour of life enlisted. In the realm of work, for instance, it will be of such quality to enable us to hold it up to God's scrutiny and to offer it to Him as the best of which we are capable. It was so at Nazareth. Think of the man in the carpenter's shop there who could affirm that every plough blade was true, every spade handle never ran a splinter into the gardener's hand – the best he was able to produce.

We can think of recreation: there will be no indulgence of a kind that might harm my brother, or my sister, or myself – and therefore it will be recreation of both body and spirit. In wealth or poverty there will be an ability to know how to abound and how to be in need; an ability to effect detachment by use, using both faithfully and so being detached properly from both. In either case, to be content, and never to be covetous, has the result that the old fears are cancelled by faith. There is a spring in the disciple's step, a song in his heart. And in the day of frightfulness, which soon will be on the world perhaps, there is no panic. A man or woman may rise in the morning and eat their breakfast and read their morning newspaper, and go out on the streets of the world and do their duty, and not be afraid. I propose therefore that when a man is living in the presence of God, the world takes on a new perspective and a new beauty.

I once knew a man in Christ who walked in the path of life more than any other I have known, and seemed to be in the presence of God in the sense I have described. I used to go walking with him sometimes, listening. He is one whom I ought to thank. One day as we were walking, he stooped and picked up a nasturtium leaf. He asked me, Did you ever see anything so marvellous, so beautiful? Then he said something that at the time seemed strange: I never noticed how beautiful a nasturtium leaf is until I came into the truth, and began to know God. He explained that as the knowledge of God deepens, so the vision of the world improves. Do you understand what he meant? A man who has come in this way into the presence of God has not lost life, he has found it. Perhaps that is what Jesus meant, "He that loseth his life for my sake shall find it" (Matthew 10:39). He discovers that the material and the spiritual are magnificently related. To a man in the presence of God there is only one world. What I mean is this: to a man in the presence of God in this sense, on the path of life, on every blade of grass is the glory of God. All the prismatic colours of the rainbow are the reflections of His majesty. This is one aspect of the path of life, and because it embraces everything we do it becomes the "fulness of joy".

If you think I have overstated this, think of something the Apostle Paul wrote, when he was talking of such people as have come to live in the path of life:

"All things are yours; whether Paul, or Apollos, or Cephas, or the world, or life, or death, or things present, or things to come; all are yours" (1 Corinthians 3:21,22). Paul says to those people who are walking on the path of life, the world is yours! That is to say, this life is utterly expansive. The path of life is not some method whereby we follow the king dragging ourselves after him in misery, and hoping that in the misery we shall gain some reward. It is a path of love, and if it entails the carrying of some cross, it ceases to be a compulsory task, and instead by the very virtue of the calling it changes our heart, as it did Simon of Cyrene, and becomes a privilege and a joy.

This is stating the ideal, of course, for this is how it is revealed to us in scripture: "And they departed from the presence of the council, rejoicing that they were counted worthy to suffer shame for his name" (Acts 5:41). The very adversity of the opposition and their suffering under it, brought them joy.

This is therefore some impression of the path of life as it has been experienced in the life of disciples: being in the presence of God step by step, and as a result discovering the fulness of joy.

Returning to Psalm 16, we must look at the next part of verse 11: "in thy presence is fulness of joy; at thy right hand there are pleasures for evermore." We have already discovered (page 49 ff.) that the right hand of God is a life encompassed by divine authority, related to God's salvation, sustained by God's strength, guided by God's activity, mastered by God's love and at last satisfied by His kingdom and His glory in the age to come. In the parable in Matthew 25, to some the Lord is going to say, "Come, ye blessed of my Father, inherit the kingdom prepared for you from the foundation of the world" (verse 34). And where are they? "On his right hand"!

"Pleasures for evermore"

At this stage we must say that there is one word in Psalm 16:11 which to some extent is a little bit embarrassing. Is it right that we are somewhat embarrassed by the word "pleasures"? We think that pleasure is a very earthly and ungodly pursuit, and rather wish the Psalmist had used a different word. We probably feel it is not the right term for the age to come, and doubtful also for the spiritual life in this world. It probably makes us feel a bit awkward.

The wonderful thing about God's world is that He used no half measures. He didn't give the birds wings, and say, You mustn't fly; He didn't give the fish fins, and say, Please don't swim; and He didn't give men appetites, and then command them not to satisfy their appetites. He didn't give man the capacity to enjoy pleasure, and then order him to be miserable. He gave man the apparatus to laugh because He intended him to laugh. In the great day to come, God will wipe away tears from off all faces, but we are nowhere told that He will suppress all laughter.

When you think carefully about the appetites God has given to men, not one of them is wrong. Every God-given appetite is legitimate; it is divinely planted and divinely approved. Sin is not the satisfying of the appetites, but the satisfying of the appetites in the wrong way. It is the achieving of lawful ends by unlawful means. Pleasure – the satisfying of the appetite – is not wrong in itself.

It is therefore possible for us to proclaim that God made man for pleasure. Readers may remonstrate that man was made for God's glory. And so he was. But think of this: man gives glory to God, and God gives pleasure to man. Think of the great manifesto of the King himself, which so often makes us realise how faulty we are, and which so often intensifies the consciousness of our failure. He began each sentence with the word, "Blessed ..." The word is *makarios* and its real meaning is 'happy'. "Happy are they that mourn: for they shall be comforted. Happy are the meek: for they shall inherit the earth ... Happy are the pure in heart: for they shall see God".

We sing a hymn which contains this phrase, "O happy band of pilgrims, if onward ye will tread ..." (hymn 381). Of course, pleasure can be wrong. What makes this good and Godly thing wrong? Worldly pleasure and wrong pleasure is abuse of the senses by forgetting the spiritual. It is the satisfying of the appetites in wrong ways. The only way to make sense of sensuality is to exercise it in harmony with God's will: never outside of it, and never in opposition. True, divinely natural pleasure is that joy which comes from the full exercise of our divinely bestowed capacities and doing it in tune with the infinite and in harmony with the eternal, looking through the material therefore to the spiritual. The man of Nazareth was the superlative example. He was a natural man in the true sense of the word. He was no recluse. Indeed, they said of him that he was "a gluttonous man, and a winebibber" (Luke 7:34). It was false of course, but it shows us that he was not an eccentric. He was concentric: true to centre, and wholly what God intended our nature to be. He was the archetypal man. He was what God meant when He said, "Let us make man in our image, after our likeness" (Genesis 1:26). This was the fulfilment, this one lonely concentric man who walked the streets and hills of Galilee; who preached in the synagogues of Judaea, and fought the first Armageddon on the green hill. He was the realisation of what God intended men should be.

Practical implications

The path of life is a life where the invisible is seen, where the inaudible is heard, where the unknowable is known. You may be saying, that's all very well, but what are the practical implications? Well, here are some of them.

Where are you going for your holidays? For if you are living in the presence of God, and if you are more and more on the path of life, it will be such a holiday as you have never had before. What of the common task and the daily round? On the path of life, in the presence of

God, hands that hitherto perhaps have hung down, bit by bit become the ministers of His mercy to others in need. Feet which ought to be beautiful, but perhaps have become unlovely because they have wandered from the way to some extent, on the path of life and in the presence of God, go at the bidding of His love in ways that bring comfort, solace, joy and blessed help to God's other children. Voices that too often have been silent and ashamed to speak are now testifying that He is the Saviour of the world.

"In thy presence is fulness of joy." That's what the Psalmist said, and part of that joy is the joy of loving service in the cause of the King. And through those on the path of life, consequently, this King of ours gains a servant – in you. He gains a witness – in you. He gains a friend – in you: somebody who will cast a little saffron on the dullness of the day; someone who will pour a little sweetness into the rancid stream of life; somebody who will throw back the frontiers of darkness in the little world in which they move; somebody who will by their aseptic influence halt the spread of corruption in the street where they live.

Have you heard the story of the missionary teaching some children in a part of the world where the word of Christ had never gone? The small group of children were round her listening to the Gospel stories recorded by Mark, and a little girl got more and more excited and agitated as the woman told her about Jesus and what he was like. The teacher had to stop and ask her what was wrong. She said, "I know that man of whom you are talking: I know him. He lives in our street". The question is very searching. Does he live in your street? That's the issue. Those on the path of life should not neglect the very things he is counting on them to achieve.

It is no good our asking for the practical implications, if we are not prepared honestly to apply them. The things we know we ought to do, but too often leave undone, are tasks that will keep us on the path of life.

Consider one final word from Psalm 16:11, the word "evermore". You can see at once that this word is a stepping stone from the world in which we live, into the world to come. It has no real meaning within the limitations of human life; it breaks through the barriers of time into eternity. "In thy right hand are pleasures for evermore". We ought to understand that eternal life is not simply a life of endless continuity; it is also a life of unsurpassed quality – as broad as it is long. When the Bible speaks of the life to come, it speaks out of the context of our present life, for there is no other way now that we could understand it. It is presented therefore as satisfying our needs, as healing our wounds, answering the cry of our hearts for true life in all its various ways and forms.

It is something which comes crying up through our very nature, for the life which we once saw in this one lonely man, and we long for it. It is always presented in terms of our own experience:

> "They that wait upon the LORD shall renew their strength; they shall mount up with wings as eagles; they shall run, and not be weary; and they shall walk, and not faint." (Isaiah 40:31)

Again, "God shall wipe away all tears from their eyes; and there shall be no more death, neither sorrow, nor crying, neither shall there be any more pain: for the former things are passed away" (Revelation 21:4).

The path of life in this world is wonderful, and there is fulness of joy, but it is not a life free from disability, or pain, or weariness. We cannot guess what it means to have fulness of joy in the world to come. However we might try to understand it, it is almost certain to be related to our present needs, disability and circumstances. It is likely to be some hope springing out of present adversity; the ending of some disability which has beset us all our life, and which only the Lord can deal with; the alleviation of some pain or the healing of some wound over which human physicians have no power; the shedding of some burden which cannot be laid down until the Lord comes and takes it away; the ending of some weariness which saps our strength and weighs down our soul; the realisation of some ideal which hasn't been satisfied – and cannot be satisfied, this side of the kingdom of God. So we are longing for the coming of the King and the beginning of the King's "evermore"; we are longing for it for a reason deep in the recesses of our human life; answering the call of life which comes singing up through our nature.

The path of life: abundant, full, infinitely and divinely wonderful, unwearied by pain, unwithered by anxiety, unsullied by sin, unended by weakness. You know, the last word has never been spoken about the meaning of the path of life in the age to come. The Bible never takes us where we are not able to go. But there are gleams in the word of God which help us to follow: here and there a flash of light. If you would catch something of its meaning, let no one rob you of the last two chapters of John's Gospel. For there we read about the one for whom Psalm 16 was first written. We see him in the splendour of the resurrection life, and hear the great whisper of the New Testament through the lips of John Zebedee, "We shall be like him". "It doth not yet appear what we shall be: but we know that, when he shall appear, we shall be like him" (1 John 3:2).

No man ought ever to be satisfied unless he is what God intended him to be, and this is where the path of life is intended to lead us finally: "We shall be like him".

So, let us be sure in our hearts of one thing: the path of life is the pathway of power. "At thy right hand there are pleasures for evermore", and in the final analysis the right hand of God is the place of authority and power. Understand this: the disciples of supreme power in the age to come will be those who are willing to accept the lowliest service now in the name, and for the sake of the King. The vision of the final joy ought to encourage us in our faithful preparation. We are the King's servants, friends by his choosing, slaves by our own volition. On the path of life therefore we are committed to the secret things. By the vision on the horizon, before long he will honour our faithfulness and heroism with pleasures for evermore.

So, let us renew our faith, and not be pessimistic about the path of life. Let us be done with lamentations about the King's business. The Truth is not yet finished. The light of the resurrection is on the pathway, on the horizon. We must sanctify ourselves today, for tomorrow the Lord will do great things for us. Today is our day, but tomorrow is the Lord's day.

God grant that we may so move upon the path of life today, that in the great tomorrow we may come at last to that wonderful fulness of joy at the right hand of God. Let us take courage: the past is gone, the present is passing, the future is certain and changeless. Paul says the future is ours, if we pursue the God-governed life; it is ours if we pursue it with faith and hope. We each need to go somewhere quietly into the presence of God, and in our hearts and in the light of His word ask how we may better seek the God-governed life. May we all, when we have thought on it, act with courage and faith in the name of the King.